The 20th Century's MOST INFLUENTIAL HISPANICS

Roberto Clemente
Baseball Hall of Famer

by William W. Lace

LUCENT BOOKS

An imprint of Thomson Gale, a part of The Thomson Corporation

Detroit • New York • San Francisco • New Haven, Conn. • Waterville, Maine • London

Picture Credits:
Cover: Focus On Sport/Getty Images; Associated Press, AP, 27, 28, 35, 47, 50, 53, 61, 65, 66, 73, 81, 87, 90; © Bettmann/CORBIS, 7, 18, 23; © Stephanie Maze/CORBIS, 11; Getty Images, 36; Focus On Sport/Getty Images, 76, 78; Hulton Archive/Getty Images, 45; Major League Baseball via Getty Images, 8, 33, 39, 69, 75, 85; Time Life Pictures/Getty Images, 40, 56, 59, 63

LIBRARY OF CONGRESS CATALOGING-IN-PUBLICATION DATA

Lace, William W.
    Roberto Clemente, baseball hall of famer / By William W. Lace.
    p. cm. — (The twentieth century's most influential: hispanics)
    Includes bibliographical references and index.
    ISBN 13: 978-1-59018-969-6 (hardcover : alk. paper)
    ISBN 10: 1-59018-969-8 (hardcover : alk. paper)
    1. Clemente, Roberto, 1934–1972—Juvenile literature. 2. Baseball players—Puerto Rico—Biography—Juvenile literature. 3. Baseball players—United States—Biography—Juvenile literature. I. Title. II. Series.
    GV865.C45L33 2007
    796.357092—dc22
    [B]

    2006017282

Printed in the United States of America

Table of Contents

Foreword

When Alberto Gonzales was a boy living in Texas, he never dreamed he would one day stand next to the president of the United States. Born to poor migrant workers, Gonzales grew up in a two-bedroom house shared by his family of ten. There was no telephone or hot water. Because his parents were too poor to send him to college, Gonzales joined the Air Force, but after two years obtained an appointment to the Air Force Academy and, from there, transferred to Rice University. College was still a time of struggle for Gonzales, who had to sell refreshments in the bleachers during football games to support himself. But he eventually went on to Harvard Law School and rose to prominence in the Texas government. And then one day, decades after rising from his humble beginnings in Texas, he found himself standing next to President George W. Bush at the White House. The president had nominated him to be the nation's first Hispanic attorney general. As he accepted the nomination, Gonzales embraced the president and said, "'Just give me a chance to prove myself'—that is a common prayer for those in my community. Mr. President, thank you for that chance."

Like Gonzales, many Hispanics in America and elsewhere have shed humble beginnings to soar to impressive and previously unreachable heights. In the twenty-first century, influential Hispanic figures can be found worldwide and in all fields of endeavor including science, politics, education, the arts, sports, religion, and literature. Some accomplishments, like those of musician Carlos Santana or author Alisa Valdes-Rodriguez, have added a much-needed Hispanic voice to the artistic landscape. Others, such as revolutionary Che Guevara or labor leader Dolores Huerta, have spawned international social movements that have enriched the rights of all peoples.

But who exactly is Hispanic? When studying influential Hispanics, it is important to understand what the term actually means. Unlike strictly racial categories like "black" or "Asian," the term "Hispanic" joins a huge swath of people from different countries, religions, and races. The category was first used by the U.S. census bureau in 1980 and is used to refer to Spanish-speaking people of any race. Officially, it denotes a person whose ancestry either descends in whole or in part from the people of Spain or from the various peoples of Spanish-speaking Latin America. Often the term "Hispanic" is used synonymously with the term "Latino," but the two actually have slightly different meanings. "Latino" refers to people only from the countries of Latin America, such as Argentina, Brazil, and Venezuela, whether they speak Spanish or Portuguese. Meanwhile, Hispanic refers to only Spanish-speaking peoples but from any Spanish-speaking country, such as Spain, Puerto Rico, or Mexico.

In America, Hispanics are reaching new heights of cultural influence, buying power, and political clout. More than 35 million people identified themselves as Hispanic on the 2000 U.S. census, and there were estimated to be more than 41 million Hispanics in America as of 2006. In the twenty-first century people of Hispanic origin have officially become the nation's largest ethnic minority, outnumbering both blacks and Asians. Hispanics constitute about 13 percent of the nation's total population, and by 2050 their numbers are expected to rise to 102.6 million, at which point they would account for 24 percent of the total population. With growing numbers and expanding influence, Hispanic leaders, artists, politicians, and scientists in America and in other countries are commanding attention like never before.

These unique and fascinating stories are the subjects of *The Twentieth Century's Most Influential Hispanics* collection from Lucent Books. Each volume in the series critically examines the challenges, accomplishments, and legacy of influential Hispanic figures; many of whom, like Alberto Gonzales, sprang from modest beginnings to achieve groundbreaking goals. *The Twentieth Century's Most Influential Hispanics* offers vivid narrative, fully documented primary and secondary source quotes, a bibliography, thorough index, and mix of color and black and white photographs which enhance each volume and provide excellent starting points for research and discussion.

Introduction

"El día más grande"

The visitors' locker room at the old Memorial Stadium in Baltimore, Maryland, was normally cramped, but the circumstances on October 17, 1971, were hardly normal. The Pittsburgh Pirates had just become baseball's champions, defeating the Baltimore Orioles 2–1 in the seventh game of the World Series. Players hugged and sprayed one another with champagne. Reporters with notebooks and broadcasters with microphones crowded around the celebrating players to get interviews.

At least one man, however, was calm. Roberto Clemente stood on a makeshift podium under the glare of television lights, a satisfied smile on his face. He had just been asked to give his reaction to being named the Most Valuable Player of the World Series. He would do so, he said, but first he wanted to give a message to his parents watching on television in his native Puerto Rico. Looking into the camera, he said in Spanish, "En el día más grande de me vida, les pido sus benediciones."[1] (On this proudest day of my life, I ask your blessing.)

In a wider sense, Clemente was speaking not only to his parents, but to everyone in Puerto Rico and even everyone of Hispanic descent. His comments in Spanish on national television reflected his enormous pride in his heritage and made a lasting impact on those who heard them. Sportswriter and author Marcos Breton remembers listening to those words, which he heard when he was just a boy: "At the time I didn't really appreciate how significant that was . . . here was this really proud man, the star of the showcase World Series, and he was addressing his people in Spanish on national television."[2]

Reason for Pride

Clemente had good reason to be proud. During the series he had collected twelve base hits in twenty-nine times at bat—a .414 average; any average over .300 was considered excellent. Five of

Roberto Clemente smiles in the Pittsburgh locker room after the Pirates won the 1971 World Series against the Baltimore Orioles.

the hits had been for extra bases, including two home runs, one in the final game. He had played his right field position flawlessly, his speed and grace more that of a teenager than a veteran of twenty seasons of professional baseball.

He was also proud because he thought that his talents were at long last getting the proper recognition. He had always believed that his accomplishments—thirteen All-Star Games and four National League batting championships—had been overlooked in favor of those of other stars, largely because he was Hispanic. Now, as always, he did not hesitate to tell reporters what he felt.

Always an inspiration, Clemente poses for a baseball portrait in this undated photo.

"I want everyone in the world to know that this is the way I play all the time," he said. "All season, every season, I gave everything I had to this game. . . . Now everyone knows the way Roberto Clemente plays."[3]

Catcher Manuel "Manny" Sanguillen, Clemente's best friend on the team, was standing nearby. "Everything he's saying is true, you know," he told reporters. "He is a great one—maybe the greatest. It is strange that he has to remind people."[4]

Leading the Way

Equally important as his performance on the field had been his influence as a team leader. After Baltimore had won the first two games of the series, Clemente kept after his teammates, urging them to keep battling and convincing them they could still win. "Clemente is carrying us,"[5] left fielder Willie Stargell had said at one point.

The World Series had brought him not only recognition, but also a forum from which he could promote a project that had long been his dream—a "sports city" for Puerto Rico. What Clemente envisioned was a facility in which young people could play and practice not just baseball but many other sports. Clemente reasoned that if a youngster could sample multiple sports, "he will like at least one of them and keep [participating]."[6]

Clemente, the son of a sugarcane field-worker, knew all about what it was like to play without a proper field or with only a makeshift ball and bat. Yet he had overcome these and other obstacles to realize his dream. Today, more than thirty years after Clemente spoke, young Puerto Ricans might benefit from exposure to any of several sports, but for Roberto Clemente—from the very first—life had been all about baseball.

Chapter 1

"God Wished It"

Clemente was a gifted athlete, as are all professional baseball players. But it was other traits nurtured during his boyhood in Puerto Rico—passion for baseball, competitiveness, supreme self-confidence, and a fierce pride in his heritage—that, combined with his physical skills, lifted him above the ordinary and made him a hero to Hispanics throughout the Americas. It was as if—as his mother later said—"he was born to play baseball."[7]

Had he not been so gifted, Clemente might well have spent his life—as did so many other Puerto Ricans—laboring in the sugar fields that formed the backbone of the island's economy. Roberto's father, Melchior, was such a man. As a *capataz*, or foreman, however, he earned considerably more than the laborers who toiled under the hot sun cutting down the sugarcane with their machetes.

Even so, Melchior was earning only about forty-five cents a day in 1934 when his youngest child, Roberto Clemente Walker was born in the San Juan suburb of Carolina. (It is customary in Puerto Rico for a son to bear his father's surname and mother's maiden name in that order.) Melchior did not earn much, but along with the money he earned selling provisions to his workers and renting out his old, much-repaired truck, plus what his wife Luisa made as a laundress, the family was provided for. Roberto would later recall that his house had five bedrooms and—an indication that the Clementes were reasonably well-off compared to most Puerto Ricans—indoor plumbing.

The house needed to be large to accommodate the Clemente family. Luisa had been a widow with three children when she and Melchior were married. And they had five more children of their own, Roberto being the youngest. Money was always tight and food sometimes scarce but, Roberto said, "We never went hungry. They always found a way to feed us."[8]

Clemente rose from humble beginnings. His father labored in a Puerto Rican sugarcane field similar to this one.

Working and Saving

One reason the Clemente family could keep food on the table was that everyone worked, including young Roberto. He earned money doing odd jobs. For example, he walked .5 mile (.8km) to fetch groceries for a neighbor, earning a penny each trip. Some of what he made went to help the family. The rest he carefully saved over three years in order to buy a secondhand bicycle.

In addition to the value of hard work, Roberto's parents taught him at least one other valuable lesson: a sense of pride and self-worth. Melchior especially, even when fatigued, projected an image of quiet dignity, looking, one observer said, "like a tired eagle."[9] He might have lifted his hat as a sign of respect when the sugar field's owner passed in his automobile, but then he would say quietly to Roberto, "He is no better than you."[10]

Playtime

As he grew, he would look for other children in the *barrio* to play [baseball] with. Sometimes I'd dress him up nice and clean, and he'd come home full of dust and mud! I'd send him to the store on an errand, and he'd be gone for hours.

— Luisa Walker de Clemente, Roberto's mother, quoted in Kal Wagenheim, *Clemente!* New York: Praeger, 1973, p. 15.

Melchior's sense of pride, so evident later in his son, involved not only wealth and social status, but also ethnicity. Puerto Rico was a melting pot, its populace largely consisting of descendants of native Indians, Spanish settlers, and Africans imported to work the plantations. While there was no overt or legal discrimination, people with lighter skin were generally given better jobs and therefore were wealthier than those with dark complexions. Many light-skinned Puerto Ricans looked down on their darker-skinned countrymen, such as the Clementes, calling them *Negritos,* or dark ones. As Luis Mayoral, who eventually became a baseball executive with the Texas Rangers, said, "Racism in Puerto Rico is worse than it is here [the United States] because it's hypocritical, it's hidden."[11]

Early Workouts

Roberto was destined to prove his equality—indeed, his superiority—on the baseball field. Long before he was actually playing organized baseball, Roberto would lie in bed for hours, listening to the San Juan Senators' Winter League games on an old radio and bouncing a ball against the walls of his room. Sometimes it was a rubber ball, bought with a few pennies from his bicycle fund. Otherwise, he might use a wad of paper held together with tape or a rolled-up pair of socks.

He would not only throw and bounce rubber balls, but would squeeze them, strengthening his hands, which grew large and powerful out of proportion to his size. "I will *always* remember his big hands," recalled Mabel Caceres, who taught in the high school Clemente attended, "those big hands that would express whatever he would not say in words."[12]

Roberto played ball with neighborhood boys and his older brothers. They had no equipment and instead had to improvise, using whatever came to hand. Roberto's first baseball glove was a bunched-up coffee bean sack. His first bat was a branch from a guava tree. Roberto spent so much time playing baseball instead of doing homework that his mother once threw the bat into the fire, only to have him pull it out.

Luisa, indeed, had dreams for her son other than a career in baseball. She envisioned him as an engineer building roads and bridges. Only later did she reluctantly come to accept the inevitable. "God wished it differently,"[13] she said.

Momen

When his older brothers participated in local softball games, Momen—Roberto's nickname coined by an older sister—tagged along. Soon he was competing equally with boys much older, joining the neighborhood team when he was eight years old. Sometimes the games would last from morning until sundown. Melchior watched one such marathon game, one in which Roberto hit ten home runs. "He played surprisingly well against boys his age or older,"[14] the father said with quiet pride.

Eventually Roberto came to the attention of Roberto Marin, who was organizing an adult amateur softball team sponsored by the rice company for which he worked as a salesman. Marin would stop in wherever he saw a neighborhood game in progress, looking for talent for his team. One evening, in San Anton, he saw a group of boys using a guava branch bat to hit a tin can crushed into the general shape of a ball.

A Good Kid

Basically, Roberto was a good kid. He did two things, played ball and stayed home. He never got into trouble. We called him Momen from the time he was little. When he had grown up and become a star, no one could remember what the name meant. He was always quiet, never got whipped. We used to kid him about that.

— Clemente's older brother Martino, quoted in Phil Musick, *Who Was Roberto?* New York: Doubleday, 1974, p. 59.

"I see this one kid . . . he never strikes out," Marin later recalled. "Bam! Bam! Bam! Tin cans all over the field. I say 'Who are you?' He say, 'I am Momen.' I told him to come to Carolina and try out for my team." [15]

Only fourteen, Roberto started at shortstop on the Sello Rice team, which included men in their twenties. Spectators loved the energy with which he played, running so fast that at times his cap would fly off—a sight that would be familiar throughout his career. Even with good speed, however, Roberto lacked the agility necessary in a shortstop. Marin moved him to the outfield, where he could run down fly balls and use his powerful arm to fire the ball back into the infield. The move suited his abilities, and he would remain an outfielder throughout his career.

High School Star

Two years later, while playing in a softball tournament, Roberto was spotted by a scout for the Juncos team in a Class AA amateur baseball league. With Marin's blessing, he switched to baseball, which unlike softball was a sport in which he might someday earn a living. He also became a standout athlete for Vizcarrondo High School, excelling not only in baseball, but also in track and field, where his ability made him a contender to compete in the Olympics.

After his junior year, however, he decided to forego high school and an opportunity for the Olympics to pursue his dream of professional baseball. As before, Marin was instrumental in his decision. "I told him that to me he looked better than the professional outfielders here in the Winter League," Marin recalled. "I told him I was going to take him to a tryout that a Brooklyn Dodger scout was going to hold in Santurce."[16]

The scout was Alex Campanis, the Brooklyn Dodgers' chief scout in the Caribbean. The tryout, sponsored by the Dodgers and the Santurce Crabbers of the Winter League, drew seventy-two young men, all hoping this would be their start toward stardom. Among them, wearing wrinkled baseball pants and a T-shirt, was seventeen-year-old Clemente.

The tryout began with each player being asked to throw a ball from the deepest part of the outfield to home plate. Many of the throws were far off-line. Others reached their target only after a few bounces. Still others reached home plate on the fly, but only after high, time-consuming arcs. Then, one throw—from Clemente—came in on a line, like a rocket, smacking against the

Puerto Rico

Loiza Aldea

San Sebastian

★ **San Juan**

Mayaguez   Castaner   Comerio

Guayama

His First Hero

Roberto Clemente's first baseball hero was Monte Irvin, who played in the Negro League in the United States and for the San Juan Senators in the Winter League in Puerto Rico. Irvin's batting style and his strong throws from the outfield were copied by Clemente when he was a boy, long before he had a chance to play organized baseball.

The high point of young Clemente's week was when his father gave him twenty-five cents on Saturday. He spent ten cents to take a bus from his home to the ballpark in San Juan and the other fifteen cents on a ticket.

Naturally shy, it took Clemente several trips before he found enough courage to ask Irvin for an autograph. Eventually they became such good friends that Clemente would carry Irvin's glove for him after a game, and the veteran player responded by giving his young fan used baseballs.

"I would [pretend] I was Monte Irvin as a kid," Clemente said years later. "I idolized him. I used to wait in front of the ballpark just for him to pass by so I could see him."

Quoted in Bruce Markusen, *Roberto Clemente: The Great One.* Champaign, IL: Sports Publishing, 1998, p. 5.

catcher's glove. Campanis looked toward the outfield. "Uno más," [17] (One more) he shouted. Again, the ball came in like an arrow.

Timing the Dash

Next Campanis timed the players in a 60-yard (55m) dash. When Clemente finished his run, the stopwatch showed 6.4 seconds. Campanis thought he had made a mistake. After all, the world record for that distance was 6.1 seconds. "Uno más," he said. Once more, his watch said 6.4 seconds.

Campanis promptly sent the other seventy-one players home, wanting to concentrate on the one he had discovered. He put Clemente in the batters' box against veteran Winter League pitcher Jose Santiago. Clemente promptly slashed line drives to all parts of the outfield. No matter where Santiago pitched to him, the inside part of the plate or the outside, the result was the same—line drives and long fly balls, ten of the latter hit out of the park.

"He was the greatest natural athlete I have ever seen as a free agent,"[18] Campanis said, a free agent being an athlete unattached and free to sign a contract with any team. The trouble was that Clemente could not sign a contract with any major-league team before his eighteenth birthday. Campanis and the Dodgers would have to wait.

The Winter League, however, was not bound by such a rule. Marin took Clemente to the home of Pedro Zorrilla, the wealthy owner of the Santurce team. Zorrilla was impressed, especially with the size of Clemente's hands, but the youngster was an unproven commodity. "I'd like to see him on the field,"[19] he told Marin.

More Impressions

Zorrilla's chance to see Clemente play came only a few days later, only he did not realize at the time that he was watching the youngster he had met. During a Crabbers exhibition game, Zorrilla saw an outfielder make two outstanding catches and an accurate throw to home plate. He called the Crabbers' manager over and asked who the player was. "That's Momen," the manager said, "a young fellow we're trying out. His last name is Clemente."[20]

Making It

I thought the Stateside players were better than Latin players. I thought you had to be Superman to make it. But when [Minnie] Minoso and [Bobby] Avila made it big, I realized that others could do it, too.

— Roberto Clemente, quoted in Arnold Hano, *Roberto Clemente: Batting King*. New York: G.P. Putnam's Sons, 1973, p. 19.

A few days later, Marin and Clemente returned to Zorrilla's home. The young player was offered his first professional contract—a four hundred dollar signing bonus and a salary of forty-five dollars a week for the ten-week Winter League season. Since he was so young, the contract had to be signed by his father.

Now a small problem arose. Melchior supported Roberto's decision to become a professional, but he thought a better deal was possible. He and Marin went to see Zorrilla, but left when the team owner said he would not increase the amount offered. The next day, Roberto came to see Marin and said he wanted the chance to play. Marin and Roberto then went to Melchior, who sensed his son's anxiety. "Tell the man," he told his son, "that I will sign for you."[21] So it was that on October 9, 1952, Melchior, who was illiterate, put his X on a contract and his son became a professional baseball player.

But just because Clemente had become a pro did not necessarily mean that he got to play much. Day after day he sat on the

A young Roberto Clemente (shown here) played for the Santurce, Puerto Rico, Crabbers from 1952 to 1957.

Béisbol in Puerto Rico

The Spanish-American War of 1898 ended Spain's rule of Puerto Rico and made the island an American commonwealth. The arrival of Americans brought baseball. After the war, hundreds of American troops were stationed in Puerto Rico. During their spare time, they formed leagues and played baseball. The game caught on among native Puerto Ricans and has had a fanatical following ever since.

The tremendous popularity of baseball among Puerto Ricans is said to date from about 1900, when a player named Amos Iglesias pitched an island team to victory over a visiting team from Cuba.

Eventually a league of professional teams—the Winter League—was formed in Puerto Rico, featuring not only home-grown players, but also stars from the Negro League and the major leagues in the United States.

Today the Winter League has become the Winter Leagues, one league each in Puerto Rico, Mexico, the Dominican Republic, and Venezuela. Each league crowns a champion that advances to the Caribbean Series. The expansion of baseball in Latin America has produced a steadily increasing number of major-league ballplayers for the United States.

bench, used only occasionally as a pinch hitter. Frustrated, he told Marin he was ready to quit. As Marin recalled, "I tell him, 'Take it easy. Your day will come.'"[22]

A Timely Hit

Clemente's day came after the halfway point in the season. Santurce had loaded the bases, but the opposing team had a left-handed pitcher on the mound. The next scheduled batter did not hit well against left-handers, so Clemente was sent up to bat. He promptly hit a long double that scored three runs and won the game for Santurce. He logged more playing time after that, but finished the season with only seventy-seven at-bats and had what was to be the lowest batting average of his long career—.234.

Things improved during the next season, particularly Clemente's hitting, thanks to help from the Crabbers' manager, Buster

Clarkson. Clarkson had noticed that each time Clemente swung, his left foot moved back toward third base, turning his body away from the plate and making it more difficult to hit pitches on the outside part of the plate. "Clarkson put a bat behind my left foot to make sure I didn't drag it," Clemente remembered. "He helped me as much as anyone."[23]

Clemente was a regular in left field that season, hitting a much-improved .288, but Zorrilla still lacked confidence in him. When the Crabbers met a Cuban team for the Caribbean championship at the end of the season, the owner signed some players from other Puerto Rican teams and left Clemente home, something the young man would never forget or forgive.

Clemente, however, soon had other things to think about. He was eighteen now, making him eligible to be signed by American teams. The Dodgers were interested, but so were the New York Giants, New York Yankees, Milwaukee Braves, and St. Louis Cardinals. The Giants were the first to make an offer, but both Clemente and Marin, his unofficial business agent, thought it too low.

Contract Offer

The Dodgers and Campanis had kept up with the youngster who had made such an impression in the tryout. They stepped in and offered a signing bonus of ten thousand dollars and a one-year contract at five thousand dollars—a huge amount of money in the eyes of the Clemente family. It was also the highest offer the Dodgers had made to anyone since Jackie Robinson, who had gone on to become a star as the first African-American player in the major leagues.

Clemente told the Dodgers he would sign with them, but Milwaukee then clouded the picture with a higher offer, a package variously reported as anywhere from twenty-eight thousand dollars to forty thousand dollars. Clemente was tempted, but his mother settled the issue. "If you gave your word," she said, "you keep your word."[24] So on February 19—with Roberto still not yet twenty-one and legally able to sign a contract—Melchior made his mark once again. Roberto was going north to play baseball, but his stay in the United States would be only long enough for spring training. His final destination was even farther north—Montreal, Canada, where Clemente would work on his game as a minor-league player.

Chapter 2

Hidden and Discovered

The 1954 season would be perhaps the most frustrating in Clemente's entire career, and those frustrations began even before the season started, when he found out he would not be playing in Brooklyn but in Montreal. It would also be a year in which he felt that his talents were being wasted and in which he would first encounter and begin a long battle against racism.

Clemente's assignment to Montreal did not mean the Dodgers lacked faith in his talent. Major League Baseball has what is known as the farm system. The big-league teams had affiliation agreements with teams at various levels in the lower or minor leagues. Players under contract to big-league teams, but who either needed more development or whose playing position was already filled at the big-league level, were assigned to a farm team, with the hope that they might build on their basic talent and thus have a better chance of excelling in the majors.

This was the case with Clemente, for multiple reasons. First, he was only nineteen years old, and since his professional experience consisted of only two years in Puerto Rico, the Dodgers thought he needed more maturity. Second, although he obviously had raw talent, team officials were unsure if it could be developed to a major-league level. "You would've had to have been a seer to predict what he would do later,"[25] Campanis said.

Great Ability

He was a wild-swinging kid, but he just radiated ability. He was a temperamental kid, and he could speak hardly any English, but luckily we had some players on the team who spoke Spanish.

— Montreal manager Max Macon, quoted in Bill Christine, *Roberto*. New York: Stadia Sports, 1973, p. 53.

Then, too, there was the Dodgers' starting outfield. Right fielder Carl Furillo had led the National League in batting the previous year. In center and left were Duke Snider and Robinson, both of whom were at the peak of their careers. Clemente would have gotten scant playing time with this trio in front of him, thus limiting his chances to improve.

Racial Limits

There perhaps was another, more subtle reason why Clemente was not immediately elevated to the Brooklyn lineup. It had been only seven years since Robinson became the first African-American to play in the major leagues since the 1800s, and racial integration was still a sensitive subject in baseball. There was an unwritten understanding that, when a team played in its home stadium, fewer than half the players—therefore a maximum of four—in the starting lineup would be black.

The way this system worked in Brooklyn was that, on days when African-American pitcher Don Newcombe was playing, one of the other blacks who usually started would be held out. Bringing another black to the team—and Clemente was considered as such because of his dark skin—would have made the situation even more complicated.

Clemente's disappointment at not being placed on the major-league roster, however, was tempered by the fact that the Dodgers thought so highly of him that they assigned him to the highest level of their minor-league system. Whereas many another nineteen-year-old rookie might have started at the A or Double-A level, Clemente went to the Montreal Royals of the Triple-A International League; this was just one step below the majors.

In assigning Clemente to the minor leagues, however, the Dodgers were running an enormous risk. Under the rules in effect that year,

The Language Problem

Roberto Clemente spoke often about the difficulties encountered by Hispanic players who did not speak English. Clemente, in fact, spoke English with a heavy accent even after more than fifteen years playing baseball in the United States.

How well he spoke English when he arrived in Montreal depends on who's telling the story. Montreal teammate Tommy Lasorda, later a Hall of Fame manager of the Los Angeles Dodgers, once said, "I had to take care of him because he couldn't speak one word of English. He couldn't go get anything to eat. . . . I'd have to take him to the restaurant and order his meals for him."

But another teammate, Joe Black, disagreed. He remembered telling Lasorda, "Tommy, why did you tell that story? . . . One, Clemente didn't hang out with you. Second, Clemente speaks English.

"Puerto Rico, you know, is part of the United States," Black said later. "So youngsters over there have the privilege of taking English in classrooms. . . . Clemente was able to communicate with those he wanted to communicate with."

Quoted in Bruce Markusen, *Roberto Clemente: The Great One*. Champaign, IL: Sports Publishing, 1998, p. 20.

Tommy Lasorda, pictured here as a member of the Kansas City Atletics in 1956, was Clemente's teammate in Montreal in 1954.

first-year players signing a contract totaling four thousand dollars or more and who did not spend the entire season on the major-league roster would be eligible to be drafted by another team.

In Hiding

Thus, by assigning Clemente to Montreal, the Dodgers knew they stood to lose him after the season. Their strategy to avoid this, apparently, was to try to keep him under wraps as much as possible so that he would escape the attention of other teams. Their approach was to keep him from batting in key situations, such as when the bases were loaded, and to adjust his playing time depending on how he was hitting. They would bench him if he was on a good streak and play him when he was in a slump.

The Desire to Play

I was impressed because he was 18 years old, just turning 19, but had a lot of desire to play. The thing that amazed me, is that sometimes one of his legs would be up in the air and he'd be hitting, and [the ball] would still go out of the ballpark. He was just *strong.*

— Montreal teammate Joe Black, quoted in Bruce Markusen, *Roberto Clemente: The Great One.* Champaign, IL: Sports Publishing, 1998, p. 18.

Clemente knew nothing of the ins and outs of the Dodgers' strategy and grew frustrated at what to him seemed the arbitrary treatment. In the first week of the Royals' season, for example, he hit a towering home run over the left field wall—the first player in team history to do so. He spent the next day on the bench. In another instance, with the bases loaded in the first inning, he was abruptly pulled and replaced by a pinch hitter.

"The idea was to make me look bad," Clemente said later. "If I struck out, I stayed in there; if I played well, I was benched. . . . I never thought I would reach such heights. Then I did . . . and they wouldn't let me play." [26]

In addition, when Clemente did get to play, it often seemed to be at the times when talent scouts from other teams were least likely to be watching. Scouts normally would watch only the first few innings of a game in order to see a team's starting players, so

Clemente often saw action as a pinch hitter in late innings or in the second game of a double-header.

Going to the Manager

As his frustrations mounted, Clemente took them to Montreal's manager, Max Macon. "He wasn't conceited," Montreal teammate Joe Black said of Clemente, "but he had a lot of self confidence and couldn't understand why he couldn't play." [27] Macon, who in later years would adamantly deny any attempt to hide his young outfielder, told him he was simply doing what he thought was best for Clemente's career.

Clemente had reasons for being unhappy away from the ball-park, as well. He had studied English in school and so, although Spanish was his native tongue, could converse somewhat with his American teammates. The dominant language in Montreal, however, was French, and Clemente knew not a word. His only close associates were three Spanish-speaking players—Black, Chico Fernandez, and Sandy Amaros. His limited English and ignorance of French made routine tasks—ordering in a restaurant or giving directions to a taxi driver—exercises in futility.

In the Hole

If you had been in Montreal that year, you wouldn't have believed how ridiculous some pitchers made him look. He had a habit of always taking a strike and getting himself in the hole with men on base.

— Montreal manager Max Macon, quoted in Phil Musick, *Who Was Roberto?* New York: Doubleday, 1974, p. 87.

Overall, however, Montreal was an attractive, friendly city. The white Canadians were tolerant of other ethnic groups, and the few blacks who lived there were not subject to segregation the way they would be in the United States. Clemente and Fernandez, in fact, shared a room in the home of a white family. "Montreal made blacks welcome then," said Black. "The white family they lived with had two teen-age daughters; that should tell you how people treated us. Like we were human beings." [28]

Such was often not the case, however, when the Royals traveled south of the border to play International League rivals in the New York cities of Buffalo, Syracuse, and Rochester and in Richmond, Virginia. It was in Richmond, especially, that Clemente first encountered overt bigotry. He could not stay in the same hotel or eat in the same restaurants with his white teammates. "I felt it was childish," [29] he said.

Light and Dark

He also observed how light-skinned Hispanics, with whom he would have mixed freely in Puerto Rico, sometimes shunned their darker-complexioned teammates, even if they were from the same country or city. "The first thing the average white Latin American player does when he comes to the States is to associate with other whites," Clemente said. "He doesn't want to be seen with Latin Negroes, even ones from his own country, because he's afraid people might think he's colored." [30]

As the 1954 season wore on, however, things got better for Clemente. On those occasions when he did get on the field, his free swinging at the plate and the flair with which he played right field captivated the Montreal fans. On one occasion, he leaped high against a wire fence to snag a ball just as it was clearing the fence for what would have been a home run. His belt snagged on the top of the fence, leaving him dangling helplessly until some cheering Royals fans freed him.

The Dodgers' efforts to keep such talent hidden from the eyes of other teams could not last forever, and eventually, by accident, the Pittsburgh Pirates discovered Clemente. Branch Rickey, Pittsburgh's general manager, was in the process of rebuilding the Pirates, who had been in decline, but without much success. Rickey sent his pitching coach, Clyde Sukeforth, to watch Montreal play a five-game series. His target was not Clemente, but Black, whom he was considering trying to acquire in a trade.

The Dodgers were going to such pains to hide Clemente that they had him take pregame batting practice with the pitchers—something few scouts bothered to watch because of pitchers' traditional inability to hit. Sukeforth, however, did bother to watch and was amazed to see a "pitcher" slamming balls out of the park.

Sukeforth eventually learned who Clemente was, but he did not get to see him play until days later when the right fielder made a brief late-inning appearance. The Pirate scout watched Clemente make a spectacular throw from the outfield and later use his speed to barely miss getting an infield hit on what should have been a routine out.

Number One Choice

That night, Sukeforth had dinner with Macon and was forthright as to Pittsburgh's intentions. "I notice you haven't been playing Clemente much lately," he said and then, before Macon could reply,

Branch Rickey (center) talks to pitcher Bob Friend (left) and infielder Dick Groat during the Pirates' spring training in 1957.

added, "You might as well use him. He's better than anyone we have in Pittsburgh right now. We're going to finish last, and we're going to draft him number one."[31] On the last day of the series, Sukeforth stopped on his way out of the ballpark to say goodbye to Macon. "Take care of our boy, Max. Make sure nothing happens to him."[32]

Macon restricted Clemente's playing time even further, and the less he played, the more frustrated he became. Macon tried to reassure him, but Clemente had had enough. On more than one occasion, he threw his uniform on the clubhouse floor and shouted that he wanted to go back to Puerto Rico.

Although no one would ever admit it, that is perhaps what the Dodgers wanted. Under baseball's rules, if a rookie player—regardless of the amount he was being paid—left his minor-league team, he could not be drafted by another major-league team. Had Clemente followed through on his threat, he would have remained under contract to the Dodgers.

Fortunately—at least from Clemente's point of view—Rickey was not about to let a potential prize slip away. He telephoned Howard Haak, a Pirate scout whose territory covered the Caribbean and who spoke some Spanish. "There's a player named Clemente up in Montreal who might be our first pick in the draft," Haak remembered Rickey saying. "Judas Priest, Sukey [Sukeforth] says he can do everything. I want you in Montreal watching him."[33]

Regular Visitor

Accordingly, Haak became a regular visitor everywhere Montreal played—home and on the road—so he was close by when, at a game in Rochester, New York, Clemente reached his breaking point. Pulled for a

Howie Haak, scout for the Pirates, had a calming influence on the temperamental Clemente.

pinch hitter even before his first time at bat, Clemente stormed into the locker room, changed clothes, and went back to the team hotel intending to pack his suitcase and return to Puerto Rico.

Haak, however, found out what had happened and went to Clemente's room. He explained to the frustrated player just what would happen if he left:

> Roberto, if you go home now you will be placed on what we call the ineligible list. Then no one will be able to pick you in the draft. You will be staying with a Brooklyn team which has all kinds of outfielders. Finish the season, then go home, and you will be playing in Pittsburgh next year, playing every day for the Pirates. [34]

Clemente listened and stayed, even though he sat on the bench for the final 25 games of the season. In fact he played in only 87 of Montreal's 154 regular-season games. He had 148 at bats, about one-fourth of what a starting player could have expected. His statistics for the year—a .257 batting average with only ten extra-base hits—reflected his sporadic playing.

Taking a Look

True to expectations, the Pirates finished last in the National League, forty-four games behind the first-place team. Rickey was almost convinced that Pittsburgh ought to use their top draft pick on Clemente, but he decided to take a look for himself. That winter he flew to Puerto Rico where Clemente was playing for Santurce in the off-season.

Rickey could not help but be impressed. Clemente was hitting over .400 and was in a race against another American big-league player, Willie Mays, for the league batting championship. After one game, Rickey asked him, "Can you do the same things in the major leagues?" Clemente replied, "I don't know. I don't know if your players in the United States are better than the ones in our country." [35]

To some, Clemente's answer to Rickey's question could have sounded arrogant, but the young player was simply being forth-right. He had never played in the major leagues and had no basis for comparison. Such bluntness—saying exactly what he was thinking—was to be a hallmark throughout his career.

Hotel Precautions

Travel—particularly sleeping in hotels—was something to which Roberto Clemente could never accustom himself, even in his earliest seasons. He claimed he slept two ways—lightly or not at all—and took extraordinary pains to make sure everything in a hotel room was just so.

The telephone, for instance, had to be exactly an arm's length from the bed so that should it ring—despite desk clerks' orders never to ring his room—he could answer the call without opening his eyes. He claimed that his eyes, once opened, would somehow be filled with tears, making it impossible for him to go back to sleep.

At every stop he would memorize the layout of his room so that he would know exactly where furniture, windows, and doors were located. "Suppose I have a nightmare and jump up," he said. "Hoo! I'm screaming and I rush through the window and the room is thirteen floors up."

After a few years in the major leagues, the Pittsburgh Pirates allowed him the rare privilege of rooming by himself. He complained that the slightest noise, no matter how careful a late-arriving roommate might be, would wake him up.

Quoted in Phil Musick, *Who Was Roberto?* New York: Doubleday, 1974, p. 182.

Rickey liked Clemente's self-confidence as well as his playing skills. So it was that on November 22, 1954, when the teams met for the draft in New York City, Pittsburgh made Clemente their first pick, gladly reimbursing the Dodgers the four thousand dollars they had paid Clemente in bonus money. Clemente was in Puerto Rico when he heard the news. "I didn't even know where Pittsburgh was,"[36] he said later. He would find out soon enough.

Chapter 3

Learning Curve

A baseball player's rookie, or first, season is usually one of the most difficult. He must compete against opponents far more talented than he has faced before. At the same time, he must try to fit in with new teammates in an unfamiliar city. For Clemente—twenty years old, knowing only a little English, new to the United States—it was especially difficult. He made it through his first year and the remainder of the 1950s, learning his craft and setting the stage for future stardom.

The year—1955—began for Clemente in one of the worst ways possible. His brother Luis died of a brain tumor on New Year's Eve. Then, as Clemente was driving home from the hospital, his car was struck broadside by a drunken driver whose speeding car had run a red light. The impact loosened three disks in Clemente's back, an injury that became a constant source of pain.

Clemente shortly encountered pain of a different sort—emotional rather than physical—when he reported for spring training in Fort Myers, Florida. Because of the segregation practiced in the American South at the time, black and white players were housed separately, and when they traveled to play other teams, had to stay in different hotels and eat in different restaurants.

"Race was something he did not have to contend with in Puerto Rico," a teammate, Nellie King, said later. "This, coupled with his native personal pride, created deep emotional problems for him." [37]

Internal Rivalry

Some of the problems arose from dynamics within the team itself. The Pirates had some aging players who resented rookies, particularly black players. "They would make 'smart' remarks about Negroes right to my face," Clemente recalled. "I didn't like some of the things the white players said to [Curt] Roberts, so I said some things they didn't like, either." [38]

Clemente also found himself at odds with some of the sportswriters covering the Pirates. The local newspaper in Fort Myers ran a story with the headline, "Puerto Rican hot dog arrives in town," [39] *hot dog* being another term for *show-off*. One writer quoted him as saying, "I no play so gut yet. Me like hot weather, veree hot. I no run fast cold weather." [40] The depiction of his accent infuriated Clemente, who thought the writers were mocking him and other Hispanics. After all, he would say, the writers never used phonetic spelling in quoting other players, such as Southern whites, with accents.

In spite of early difficulties off the field, Clemente hit well in spring training—a .395 average. Still, the young slugger was on the bench for the Pirates' first three regular-season games. Clemente's first start came on April 17, and he immediately made an impression, getting a base hit in his first at bat and a total of nine hits in his first week.

By June, Clemente was among the top hitters in the National League. Still, opposing pitchers had spotted two weaknesses. He swung at too many bad pitches and, when swinging, would bob his head up and down, which sometimes caused him to lose sight of the pitch. As a result, within a ten-day period his batting average fell from .315 to .275.

Boiling Over

Clemente took no pains to hide his frustration. Many times, after striking out, he would hurl his plastic batting helmet into the dugout, cracking it. He stopped only when the Pittsburgh manager, Fred Haney, fined him the cost of the helmets—ten dollars each.

While his hitting was suspect, Clemente's defensive play was spectacular. His speed enabled him to field fly balls that otherwise would have been extra-base hits, and it quickly became known that he had one of the strongest, most accurate throwing arms in baseball. Many

Pirates rookie Clemente poses with his bat for an official Major League Baseball photo in 1955.

an opposing player trying to take an extra base—stretching a single into a double or a double into a triple—found a Pittsburgh infielder waiting with the ball, thanks to powerful throws by Clemente from the outfield. Indeed, more than forty years later, a 1997 magazine article rated him as having the best arm in baseball history and a player "who defined the art of intimidating base runners."[41]

Natural Talent

He was inexperienced, but you could see the natural talents of speed, powerful body and a magnificent throwing arm. He just knocked your eyes out with the things he could do.

— Pittsburgh teammate and later broadcaster Nellie King, quoted in Bruce Markusen, *Roberto Clemente: The Great One.* Champaign, IL: Sports Publishing, 1998, p. 40.

Still, Clemente's rookie season was a difficult one. He missed twenty-seven games, many of them with injuries about which he complained loudly, to the annoyance of his teammates. He began to acquire a reputation as someone who would invent or imagine injuries.

Clemente's life off the field was difficult, as well. Other than fellow outfielder Roman Mejias, he had only one close friend—an African American postal worker named Phil Dorsey. Clemente had been introduced to Dorsey by teammate Bob Friend, who thought Dorsey might be of some help. Dorsey arranged for Clemente and Mejias to save money by renting a room in a private home rather than living in a hotel. He helped Clemente shop for clothes and took him to movies, something the young Puerto Rican enjoyed and that helped him improve his English.

Fan Friendly

Clemente was popular, however, with the Pittsburgh fans. This was not only because of his flashy style of play but also because of his willingness to remain outside the ballpark after the games, sometimes for as long as two hours, signing autographs. It was not that Clemente loved the attention, but because he really did not have anything else to do. "I was lonely," he said years later. "Why not sign? People remember you if you are nice to them."[42]

*Clemente demonstrates his superb skills in right field during a
1958 Pirates game against the Chicago Cubs.*

Many of those fans seeking autographs were teenage girls,
although Clemente did not form relationships with them. "He
was good-looking and single," Dorsey recalled. "As far as going
out on dates, he was normal, but there was no one special he went
out with. His mind was set on playing baseball."[43]

Nevertheless, Clemente had reason to be glad to see the 1955 season end. Moreover, the end of the season brought some changes that favored him. Rickey retired as general manager and was replaced by Joe Brown. Brown, in turn, dismissed Haney as field manager and brought in Bobby Bragan.

Brown made other personnel changes, releasing many veteran players to make way for younger ones. Highly promising players such as Bill Mazeroski, Dick Groat, and Bill Virdon joined the team. Bragan's contribution was a change in attitude among the players. He would tolerate no mental mistakes, as Clemente found out after the second game of the season when he was fined twenty-five dollars for missing a signal ordering him to bunt.

The players responded to the new discipline with a spirit that carried over into the locker room. Factionalism, which had been a problem for much of 1955, largely disappeared, thanks mostly to first baseman Dale Long, who became the team leader. Long settled arguments before they became too divisive and made players discuss conflicts with one another openly instead of talking behind someone's back.

"Arriba!"

The Pirates' new look and new attitude began to pay off. In mid-June they were in first place, and Clemente was hitting .357—third best in the league. Such offense, combined with his sparkling defensive play, made him an increasing favorite with the fans, who began to shout "Arriba!"—a Spanish word loosely translated as "On your feet!" In July, a Pittsburgh reporter wrote, "The fans discovered a new hero—right-fielder Roberto Clemente."[44]

The sudden surge of success, however, was not to last, either for the Pirates or for

Joe Brown (pictured) succeeded Branch Rickey in 1955 as Pirates general manager.

Birth of a Nickname

In recent years, new major-league teams tend to choose their nicknames through a contest or have them picked out by a marketing expert. When professional baseball was just beginning, though, nicknames sometimes just came along and stuck.

Pittsburgh's team is one of the oldest, having been founded in 1884, and was first known as the Alleghenies, after the nearby mountain range. Three years later Louis Bierbauer, a star player for the Philadelphia Athletics, Pittsburgh's fiercest rival, signed a contract with a team in a new league, the Players' League, which soon went bankrupt.

The Athletics and their fans expected Bierbauer to return to Philadelphia, but he surprised them by going to Pittsburgh. An enraged Philadelphia sportswriter compared the incident to "piracy on the high seas." From then on, the Pittsburgh team was known as the Pirates. They are also unofficially known as the Buccaneers, often abbreviated as "Bucs" for the convenience of headline writers who have limited space in which to squeeze words.

Clemente. In late June, the team lost eight straight games and began a long slide down the standings. Clemente, meanwhile, cooled off at the plate, although he still finished with a solid .311. For whatever reason he did not have as much trouble with injuries, missing only seven games. For at least once in his career, nobody accused him of imagining illnesses or injuries. As a team, the Pirates finished with sixty-six victories, six more than in 1955. But more important, for the first time since 1951, they were not in last place.

Clemente's outstanding season earned him a hero's welcome when he returned to Puerto Rico to play winter ball. It also had earned him a healthy raise in salary, and he celebrated by buying his parents a house costing $12,500, a huge amount for Puerto Rico in the 1950s. In Clemente's mind, the house was not a gift. "I am trying to pay them back for giving me so much,"[45] he said.

Back Trouble

Clemente's good hitting carried over into Winter League play. He finished the season with a .396 average and won the league batting championship by sixty points. His success, however, came at a cost. He had begun having more back trouble during the major-league season, and playing a full season of winter ball did not give his back a chance to rest. The back problems flared up anew during spring training of 1957, and he had to sit out several exhibition games.

Media Troubles

Some of them [sportswriters] put words in your mouth and that's what they did to him when he was young. . . . He was just learning to handle the language and he couldn't express what he felt or thought and it frustrated him. Writers who couldn't speak three words of Spanish tried to make him look silly.

— Bill Mazeroski, "My 16 Years with Roberto Clemente." *Sport,* November, 1971, p. 63.

The Pirates' medical staff tried all sorts of remedies—ultrasound, heat, injections—but nothing worked. On the opening day of the season, Mejias was in right field and Clemente on the bench.

When he did finally get into the lineup, he was a shadow of what he had been the previous year. Every hard swing brought a stab of pain. Team doctors took X-rays but found nothing wrong. One doctor even said that taking Clemente's tonsils out might help. It did not.

As he missed more and more games, Clemente's teammates once again began to whisper that his injuries were all in his mind, that he really did not want to play. Even Bragan, one writer reported, "thinks Clemente's back ache is more mental than lumbar [a section of the spine]."[46] Clemente protested, saying, "Bragan know I like to play . . . that I get sick when I see somebody play and I cannot."[47]

Thoughts of Quitting

When the season finally ended, it was none too soon. The Pirates tied for last place, Bragan was fired, and Clemente had posted the lowest batting average of his major-league career—.253—while missing forty-three games. He thought about quitting. "I gonna rest [during the winter]," he said. "If the pain is still there, I won't come back to spring training."[48]

He almost kept his promise to rest. He played winter ball, but he went up to bat only 32 times as opposed to 225 at bats the previous winter. The respite apparently did him some good, because he started the 1958 season strong, hitting almost .400 during the first month. Then injury struck again. This time it was not in his back, but in his throwing arm.

On April 30, during a game against the Dodgers, Clemente made a sidearm throw and heard a cracking sound in his right elbow. "It feels like needles in there," he said, "so I don't throw [hard] until I have to."[49] He began to sit out a game now and then when the pain was too much, and this drew the ire of the Pirates' new manager, Danny Murtaugh.

Clemente (number 21) takes a swing at a pitch by Brooklyn Dodgers pitcher Don Drysdale during a 1956 game.

Murtaugh, according to King, was tough and expected others to be tough, too. Murtaugh, King notes, "came up the hard way. You know, one of these guys who chew tobacco and spit on their injuries. I think there was quite a misunderstanding between Clemente and him." [50] Worse, Murtaugh did not try to disguise his skepticism about Clemente's injuries. At one point, when Clemente was out of the lineup with a recurrence of back pain, Murtaugh yelled, "You're faking the injury. . . . Take off the uniform," whereupon Clemente yelled back, "No one takes off my uniform while I'm playing for the Pirates." [51]

Season's End

Clemente endured Murtaugh's wrath, often playing when he did not feel well. He finished with a season that, although not great, was at least respectable. His batting average was .289, and he led all National League outfielders with twenty-two assists throwing base runners out. The Pirates made even greater strides, winding up in second place with a record of eighty-four wins and seventy losses.

One reason that Clemente was able to maintain his emotional equilibrium despite his run-ins with Murtaugh was that he had become much more used to life in the United States. He was no longer a stranger in Pittsburgh but a recognized figure. He learned to relax, usually by listening to an extensive collection of classical music—an interest few associated with a professional athlete. Brown, for one, was able to see

Pirates manager Danny Murtaugh (pictured) was often at odds with Clemente.

beyond Clemente's athletic prowess. "Nobody ever recognizes how very, very smart he was—intelligent," Brown said years later. "He had a perception, an intellect that was somewhat unusual."[52]

The Mechanic

He could have been hypocritical and gone and played [with injuries]. But no one then seemed to realize the sensitivity he had for his body. He looked at it the way a mechanic looks at a racing car. If it wasn't right, he wanted to tune it. . . . The only thing that dictated what Clemente did was what he felt was right.

— Pittsburgh teammate and later broadcaster Nellie King, quoted in Phil Musick, *Who Was Roberto?* New York: Doubleday, 1974, p. 103.

This year, when the season ended, there was no thought of Clemente playing Winter League ball in Puerto Rico. He had an appointment on a different island—Parris Island, South Carolina, the location of a Marine Corps boot camp. Like many professional athletes his age, Clemente was subject to the military draft. Instead of waiting to be drafted, however, he had chosen to enter the Reserves, which entailed a six-month tour of duty. Much of that duty involved rigorous physical training. When he finished his six months, Clemente felt stronger, had gained ten pounds, and even believed his back problems had disappeared. When asked how that could be, he answered, "I worked like hell."[53]

High Expectations

As healthy as he had been since his rookie year, Clemente's expectations were high. So were those of the Pirates and their fans. The team had been at or near the top of the standings most of the previous season, and there was a feeling in Pittsburgh that 1959 would bring the first league championship since 1927.

The high hopes remained unfulfilled, both for the Pirates and Clemente. Everything that had gone right the previous year seemed to go wrong. Fly balls that once dropped for base hits were caught by opposing players. Pitcher Friend, who had won twenty-two games, won only eight. The team finished with a record of 78–76, a distant fourth place behind the Dodgers.

Choosing a Number

Shortly before the opening of the 1955 major-league season, Roberto Clemente's first with the Pittsburgh Pirates, he still had not selected a uniform number. It was an important decision for the young Puerto Rican, and he found it hard to make up his mind.

The story goes that Clemente and his new friend, Phil Dorsey, went to a movie in Pittsburgh a few days before the first game. On impulse, Clemente picked a scrap of paper from the theater floor and printed his full name—R-O-B-E-R-T-O C-L-E-M-E-N-T-E W-A-L-K-E-R. He counted the number of letters—twenty-one—and informed the Pirates' equipment manager the next day that 21 was the number he wanted. It was the number he wore the rest of his career.

In spite of the fact that, according to Puerto Rican custom, his father's surname—Clemente—preceded his mother's—Walker—he would always be known in the United States as Robert Walker Clemente, because some youngsters are given their mother's original surname as their middle name.

As for Clemente, his good health lasted only a month. On May 17 he was hit by a pitch on the right elbow, the same one that had bothered him the previous year. The bone was chipped, and the chips caused a painful inflammation that kept him out of the lineup until July 5. When he returned, he was so impaired by the elbow and a recurrence of back problems that his batting average fell at one point to .176.

He rallied during the last part of the season and finished with a decent average of .296. The problem, however, for Clemente, the team, and the fans was whether decent was good enough. His batting average over five seasons was .282. That was respectable but certainly not what Clemente wanted and not what the Pirates had expected when they drafted him.

Both the player and the team had hopes that a breakthrough year was just around the corner in 1960. They were both correct, but what brought baseball's ultimate joy to Pittsburgh would bring more frustration to Clemente.

Chapter 4

The Making of a Superstar

After five years in the major leagues, Clemente had yet to attain the greatness the Pittsburgh Pirates had hoped for and that he so greatly wished for. The next two seasons would see a full flowering of his talent, but he would not yet receive—at least in his own view—the recognition he deserved.

Clemente entered the 1960 season in a good frame of mind, having played a full season of winter ball in Puerto Rico with a .330 batting average. More important, he was injury free—or as injury free as he would ever claim to be. "I am mad at my back and my arm when they hurt, and I am worrying very much,"[54] he told Pittsburgh writer Joe King. He then demonstrated to King that when he shifted his back, an audible "click" could be heard, produced by loose spinal disks.

Clemente's teammates had reason to shake their heads and roll their eyes at one another. Time after time they had listened to him talk about how much he was hurting, only to see him go out on the field and play spectacularly. In 1957, the *Sporting News* had written, "The case history of Clemente is the worse he feels, the better he plays," and the article went on to quote Bragan as saying, "I'd rather have a Clemente with some ailment than a Clemente who says he feels great with no aches for pains."[55]

Playing with Injuries

He played with injuries other guys wouldn't have come to the ballpark with because he knew his presence made a difference. . . . One year he had a bad knee, all swollen and stiff. I told him not to play, that he could be out for weeks if he did. . . . 'No, we need a few wins,' he said. And that kind of thing was not unusual.

—Pittsburgh Pirates trainer Tony Baritrome, quoted in Phil Musick, *Who Was Roberto?* New York: Doubleday, 1974, p. 189.

Hurting or not, Clemente got off to one of the fastest starts of his career in 1960. He was named National League Player of the Month for May after batting .336 with twenty-five RBIs (runs batted in) in twenty-seven games. Writers and broadcasters speculated that he might become the first player to hit .400 since Ted Williams did it in 1941. Clemente played down such talk. "Nobody will ever hit .400," he would say later. "We play too many games. We don't rest enough."[56]

Hot Streak

The Pirates started off as hot as Clemente had. On April 21 they won their ninth straight game, their longest winning streak in fifteen years. Three days later they moved into first place and began to sense that perhaps this was their year. Certainly it was proving to be a year when the breaks finally fell their way. They would win twenty-one games in their last at bat, twelve after two men were out in the final inning.

The fans were getting a whiff of destiny, too. They came to watch in record numbers, and by the start of June, more children had been reported lost than all the previous season, as their parents became too absorbed by the game to keep an eye on them. A new chant, "Beat 'em, Bucs," was heard, bucs being the shortened form of buccaneer, or pirate.

The crowds' enthusiasm affected the players. "The fans cheer when you strike a guy out. They explode when an easy fly ball is hit to the outfield," said Friend. "You'd never know they've had baseball here for sixty years."[57]

Clemente's torrid spring continued into summer, and he was hitting .333 at the end of June. Writers began calling him another Mays, comparing him to the Giants' star, but even such a compliment stung Clemente's pride. "Willie is a very good ball player," he

Making the most of his hot streak, Clemente shows off his speed as he runs toward first base in a Pirates game.

said, "but why does everybody say I run like Willie, catch like Willie, throw like Willie, and hit line drives like Willie. I am not Willie. I am Roberto Clemente."[58]

Hero to Hispanics

One group that had long appreciated Clemente for himself was the small but vocal Hispanic population in Pittsburgh. In 1960, however, he began to draw fans outside Pittsburgh, especially in cities that had large Puerto Rican populations. A Chicago Cubs fan recalled that, sitting in the right field bleachers in Wrigley Field, "we're surrounded by Puerto Ricans yelling, 'Arriba! Arriba!' And every inning Clemente comes near the wall to talk with them in Spanish. The joy in the young boys' faces as their fathers laughed with Clemente."[59]

Second to None

A throwing arm virtually second to none. If it was second to anyone, it would have been Rocky Colavito for sheer power. But Clemente's arm for accuracy and throwing with authority from right field absolutely would change the outcome of a game.

— Sportswriter John Steadman, quoted in Bruce Markusen, *Roberto Clemente: The Great One.* Champaign, IL: Sports Publishing, 1998, p. 268.

There was joy in the Pirates' locker room, too. Several players other than Clemente were having banner years. Groat was on his way to a .325 batting average, highest in the National League. Pitchers Vern Law and Friend would win twenty and eighteen games, respectively. Relief pitcher ElRoy Face would save twenty-four games by substituting for the starting pitcher and preserving the Pirates' lead. The days of clubhouse cliques and bickering were over, at least for a time. "To win, you must play as a family," Clemente later said. "We played as a family."[60]

The season was going so well that everyone on the team took pains to avoid doing something they thought might cause a change of fortune. Superstitions among professional athletes were—and are—common. A player performing exceptionally well may keep his pregame routine precisely the same to avoid doing anything

Clemente robs the Giants' Willie Mays of a possible hit during a game. Despite such outstanding plays, the MVP award eluded Clemente for years.

that might change his luck—eating exactly the same meals, parking his car in exactly the same spot, and so forth.

Superstitions

No one on the 1960 Pittsburgh team had more superstitions than Clemente. Once, when a small band that played at home games followed the team to Chicago, the Pirates lost two games. When the team returned to Pittsburgh, recalled teammate Mazeroski, Clemente said, "Keep that band out of here. Every time they play we get beat." Mazeroski also revealed that when the Pirates won a game, Clemente would wear the same uniform shirt the following day and would neither change it—nor wash it—until the team lost. "We had a *hell* of a time this year when we won eleven straight games!"[61] Mazeroski said.

Whatever Clemente was doing, it seemed to be working. He was hitting more consistently and driving in more runs than ever before. He had never been known as a power hitter, but he would finish the season with sixteen home runs, ten more than in any previous year. In the field, he led all National League outfielders in assists.

Sportswriters and broadcasters around the country began to take notice of Clemente's performance. He was increasingly mentioned as a prime candidate for the annual National League Most Valuable Player award as selected by the Baseball Writers Association of America. In July, he was told by the St. Louis Cardinals' Stan Musial, a three-time winner of the award, "If you don't win the MVP award this year, you never will."[62]

Clemente was soon to learn, however, that a prominent member of the Baseball Writers Association, Les Biederman of the *Pittsburgh Press,* was working against him. Biederman had sent a letter to association members enlisting their support for Clemente's teammate Groat for the award. In fact, Biederman listed Clemente as only the third most-deserving member of the Pirates behind Groat and third baseman Don Hoak.

Championship Run

However, the award was not due to be announced until November. Meanwhile there was a league championship to be won. Clemente was brilliant both at bat and in the field. He saved one game in San Francisco, leaping to catch a fly ball and doing so just before crashing into a concrete wall and gashing his chin. After five stitches and only one day of rest—a week had been suggested by doctors—he was back on the field.

The Pirates clinched the National League championship on September 25 while playing in Milwaukee. Clemente was at bat when he heard cheers from the Pittsburgh dugout. News had just been received that the second-place St. Louis Cardinals had lost and thus had been mathematically eliminated from contention. Clemente singled and then, after a double by Hal Smith, ignored a signal to stop at third base and headed for home plate, just beating the throw. Asked later why he ignored the signal, he said, "Stop at third? I want to get to the bench quick and talk about winning the pennant."[63]

The next step would be the World Series against the American League champion New York Yankees, against whom the Pirates were given little chance by experts. Led by stars such as Mickey

Mantle, Roger Maris, and Bill "Moose" Skowron, the Yankees were in the middle of a ten-year span that would see them win the American League nine times.

Yet in the first game of the series, played in Pittsburgh, the Pirates won, 6–4, breaking a fifteen-game New York winning streak. The next day, however, saw the Yankees pound out six extra-base hits, including two home runs by Mantle, to win easily, 16–3.

Setting the Tone

The first two games set the tone for the series. The Yankees would win the third and sixth game by a combined score of 22–0, but the Pirates managed to squeeze out victories of 3–2 and 5–2. Clemente had been a major contributor, batting .320 and getting at least one hit in every game.

The stage was thus set for what many experts rate as the best seventh and deciding game in World Series history. Clemente contributed one of the key plays, coming to bat in the eighth inning with two runners on base, two men out, and the Pirates trailing, 7–5. He swung hard at a Jim Coates pitch, but managed only a slow ground ball to the left of first base for what appeared to be the final out. Skowron fielded the ball and tossed it to Coates, who was running over to step on the base. Clemente's speed, however, paid off, and he beat Coates to the base.

Maintaining an Image

Robby loves his image. He takes good care of it. He is wary of being with people he does not approve of. He believes people know you by the company you keep, so he keeps careful company. . . . But he is a great player. If he were on the Yankees, Mickey Mantle would be nowhere. That's how good he is.

— Teammate Alvin McBean, quoted in Arnold Hano, *Roberto Clemente: Batting King.* New York: G.P. Putnam's Sons, 1973, p. 130.

One run scored on the play and the next batter, Smith, hit a three-run home run to put the Pirates ahead 9–7. New York was not finished, however, scoring two runs in the first half of the ninth inning to tie the score. But Pittsburgh's first hitter in the last

Fans and teammates mob Pittsburgh second baseman Bill Mazeroski on the field after his home run wins the World Series against the Yankees in 1960.

of the ninth, Mazeroski, homered to left field, and the Pirates were world champions.

Clemente celebrated with his teammates on the field and, for a brief time at least, in the locker room afterward. His actions after the game, however, have been debated. According to Clemente, he dressed quickly and left the stadium because he wanted to celebrate with the fans. "I come out of the clubhouse and saw all those thousands of fans in the streets," he said later. "I did not feel like a player at the time. I felt like one of those persons, and I walked the streets among them."[64]

Another Version

Bill Nunn, a sportswriter who was closer to Clemente than any other, gave a less positive picture of Clemente's postgame actions. According to Nunn, Clemente did not want to be a part of the celebration and, in the locker room, asked him, "Hey, how about getting me out of here?"[65] Nunn said that he then drove Clemente to the airport where he boarded a plane for Puerto Rico.

Clemente's abrupt departure was widely criticized in the newspapers, and some writers speculated that he was upset because he felt he had received less attention, both during the World Series and the regular season, than he deserved. Others speculated that he was having problems with some of his teammates. "He was sort of an outsider on the team," writer Roy McHugh said. "He didn't mix well with the older players."[66]

Clemente had even more reason to be upset in November, when he learned that Groat, indeed, had been voted the Most Valuable Player in the National League. He was disappointed that he had finished in the voting behind Groat, but he was infuriated that seven other players finished ahead of him. "I never say Groat should not win it," he said. "I feel like I should not be close to tenth. I led the club in RBI's with ninety-four . . . but in the [World] Series, you need a magnifying glass to see my name in the papers."[67]

The perceived slight would gnaw at Clemente for years. "I was very bitter," he said long afterward. "I am still bitter. I'm a team player . . . winning the pennant and the world championship were more important than any average, but I feel I should get the credit I deserve."[68]

Clemente was convinced that the baseball writers had voted Groat and two other Pirates—Law and Hoak—ahead of him because he was Hispanic and they were white. "He was convinced that it was due to that [racism]," recalls baseball executive Luis Mayoral. "To the day of his death he was convinced of that."[69] As a result, the season that should have been so sweet left a sour taste. When his world championship ring arrived, he vowed never to wear it. He kept that promise.

Keeping a Promise

Clemente would keep another promise made after the 1960 season. Stung by having received less acclaim than he felt due him, he told his parents that he would make himself the best hitter in baseball—so good that he could not possibly be overlooked again.

He reported for 1961 spring training full of determination and received help from someone who could turn hope into reality. George Sisler, the Pirates' hitting coach, advised him to use a heavier bat. By switching from a 31-ounce (873g) bat to one as heavy as 36 ounces (1021g), Sisler said, Clemente's swing would become more controlled. Greater control, Sisler argued, would help him make better contact with the ball, even if the bat was not traveling as fast. The result would be more power. There was no reason, Sisler said, why Clemente could not become the best hitter in baseball.

Clemente followed Sisler's advice, and the results showed how sound it was. By the mid-season All-Star Game break, Clemente was

The Visualization Technique

Often during his career Roberto Clemente's teammates would find him, prior to a game, stretched out on a trainer's table with the room lights off. Sleeping? No, visualizing.

"A lot of players do this," said teammate Nellie King. "He'd turn the lights out when he'd go in there. He said to me, 'You know what I do when I go in there? Everybody thinks I am hurting, or there is something wrong with my back again. [But] if [St. Louis' Bob] Gibson is pitching that day, I will lay down and I will bat against Bob's pitches four times before I play the game. I will see his fastball come inside and I'll see his slider go away and the curveball, and I will poke the ball to left field. . . . I will bat four times [in my mind] and I will get four hits before I go out there, but I have seen every pitch he has. And on a good day, I go out there and see that pitch that I've already hit, so I hit it.'

"I think there's a lot of guys who do that," King said. "A lot of sports people do it, but he really had it down to a dedicated [science]."

Quoted in Bruce Markusen, *Roberto Clemente: The Great One.* Champaign, IL: Sports Publishing, 1998, p. 138.

In May 1965, Clemente bats as a pinch hitter in the ninth inning in a game against the Chicago Cubs.

hitting .367 and had batted in fifty-one runs. In the All-Star Game he scored one run and batted in two, including the game winner. He was so proud of his performance that it would be his 1961 All-Star ring he would wear afterward instead of the World Series ring.

But if Clemente was having a better year in 1961, his team-mates were not. Law, who had won twenty games the year before, developed arm trouble and could post only three victories. Groat's average fell to .275. The close games the Pirates had won the year before now tended to go the other way.

Clubhouse Feuds

The camaraderie in the clubhouse disappeared along with the victories. Hoak sharply and publicly criticized first baseman Dick Stuart for what he thought was a lack of effort, and an argument between Stuart and Friend almost resulted in a fight.

Clemente's Cocktail

Few sports stars fretted about their health more than Roberto Clemente, whose entire career was a laundry list of aches and breaks, pains and sprains. One of the methods he used to keep himself healthy was downing a drink of his own making, and how he made it depended on what sorts of ingredients were on hand. Raw eggs were a basic element, sometimes a dozen at a time. To them he might have added sugar, any kind or combination of fruit or fruit juices, and crushed ice. Then he would mix them all in a blender and serve it up.

A friend, Luis Mayoral, once was convinced to try one such concoction. "He'd take grape juice, and then he'd put like twelve eggs in there and beat it," Mayoral recounted. "He always told me, 'This is what keeps me strong.' And between you and me, it tasted like [bleep]. Man, that tasted bad, but I drank a glass or two. He even took pride in fixing that punch."

Quoted in Bruce Markusen, *Roberto Clemente: The Great One*. Champaign, IL: Sports Publishing, 1998, p. 293.

Clemente, however, seemed to have earned everyone's respect. Instead of talking behind his back about his eternal complaints of injuries, they needled him in a friendly manner about his smoldering resentment over the MVP voting, calling him "Mr. No Votes."

Despite, or perhaps because of, the teasing of his teammates, Clemente kept up his hitting pace. During one week in late July, he collected twenty hits in thirty-six times at bat—a .556 average. He reached a high mark of .371 on August 6 and eventually ended the season at .351, the beat average in the National League and second in the major leagues only to Norm Cash of Detroit at .361.

The Pirates had not fared as well, finishing in sixth place, eighteen games behind the Cincinnati Reds. It would be another decade before another championship would come their way. Clemente, however, was just reaching the top of his game. Many more years lay ahead of him—years during which he would not only be hailed as a star, but would emerge as a leader and role model for developing Hispanic players.

Chapter 5

The Road to the MVP

With his stellar seasons in 1960 and 1961, Clemente could not have been blamed for thinking his hopes for recognition by the nation's sportswriters were shortly to be realized. Instead, it would take five more banner years before the rest of the baseball world acknowledged what Clemente knew in his heart. In the meantime, he became more mature, both as a player and as a person, gradually taking on the mantle of leadership for Hispanics in the major leagues.

If he had hoped to pick up in 1962 where he had left off, however, he was disappointed. He reported to spring training complaining of weakness and 10 pounds (4.5kg) lighter than normal. Doctors put his condition down to "nervous stomach." This, plus an operation to remove bone chips from his elbow, but which failed to find any bone chips, led to renewed talk that Clemente tended to imagine illnesses.

His performance, however, showed that something was wrong. By late May he was batting only .256, although he rallied during the summer and was hitting .336 by the time he was chosen for the National League All-Star Game team. He finished the year at

.312, eighth best in the league, but his home run total fell from twenty-three to ten.

It was not a particularly good season either for Clemente or the Pirates, who finished fourth. As usually happens when a team is losing, tempers were on edge. Relations were especially strained between Clemente and Murtaugh. On one occasion Murtaugh accused Clemente of loafing, not running fast enough after hitting a ground ball even though Clemente was playing despite having two stitches in an ankle, the consequence of an earlier injury.

Confrontation

When Clemente said he was too injured to continue the game, Murtaugh ordered him to take his usual spot in right field. Clemente refused, and the manager told him he would be fined

Danny Murtaugh strides onto the field in Pittsburgh during a game in the 1960 World Series against the Yankees.

$150 if he failed to obey. Clemente refused to take the field, and the fine escalated to $650 before Murtaugh gave up in disgust.

The scene was typical of many between player and manager. Murtaugh thought players should perform despite injury and without complaint. Clemente, however, said he was only being honest. "If I'm sick," he said, "I do not deny. If my back is hurting and I am forced to punch at the ball, with no power, I tell the truth. I tell them I am hurting."[70]

Things That Matter

I recall a number of times when people were having problems, and he would sit people down, including myself, and just go over things, that baseball is not everything, it's your family and how you get along with people that are more important.

— Teammate Dave Giusti, quoted in Bruce Markusen, *Roberto Clemente: The Great One*. Champaign, IL: Sports Publishing, 1998, p. 234.

Tensions between the two continued throughout the next season, which would be, in general manager Brown's words, "a nightmare."[71] Brown had tried to revive the team by trading older players such as Groat, Stuart, and Hoak for younger talent. The newcomers did not work out as planned, and the Pirates finished twenty-five games behind the champion Dodgers.

In addition to his regular run-ins with Murtaugh, Clemente began to complain frequently and publicly about how he was treated by umpires. "Every year I lose fifteen to twenty [batting average] points on close plays at first base," he said. "I seldom argue unless I feel the umpire is wrong, I have a good record at the league office, but this is the worst year for umpiring I have ever seen."[72]

Bumping the Ump

Clemente's worst confrontation with an umpire came when, while protesting a close play, he—accidentally, he claimed—bumped umpire Bill Jackowski. Clemente was ejected from the game and fined $250 by the league office. He filed a formal protest, but it was denied. Years later Clemente admitted he had been wrong, but he added that Anglo umpires should be more understanding of Hispanic temperaments. "We Latins get more excited than Americans," he said. "We have a lot of pepper blood. Sometimes I don't think Americans understand this."[73]

Clemente, in fact, was speaking out more and more on behalf of all Hispanics in the major leagues, something he was able to do from the vantage point of a veteran star. "To me, he had the intestinal fortitude to become the spokesman for Latinos in the game," said Mayoral. "There have been other Latinos prior to him like Minnie Minoso and Chico Carrasquel—great players, great individuals—but they didn't really have that makeup to really take the flag and lead Latinos in searching for recognition and respect in major league baseball."[74]

One area in which Clemente spoke out, not surprisingly, was the difference he perceived in the way Hispanics were treated when ill or injured compared to white players under similar circumstances. "If a Latin player is sick," he said, "they [managers] say it is all in the head. They act like we are lazy, like we don't want to play."[75]

A Likable Guy

One thing stood out. Through all the outbursts [at reporters] and the arguments and controversies, it was almost impossible not to like the guy. I can remember the first time as a rookie that I had to interview him. He was polite and pleasant, as though he sensed my anxiety and was trying to make it easier for me.

— Sportswriter Ira Miller, quoted in Phil Musick, *Who Was Roberto?* New York: Doubleday, 1974, p. 133.

Most of his comments, however, were aimed at trying to get across to baseball officials how difficult it was for players from the Caribbean and South America to adjust to life in the United States. "Latin Americans need time to get adjusted," he said. "We lead different lives in the United States. . . . Everything is strange. . . . We Latins are people of high emotions, and coming to this country we need time to settle down emotionally. Once we're relaxed and have no problems, we can play."[76]

Clemente, who blamed his hot temper on his Latin "pepper blood," heatedly argues with an umpire over a call in 1960.

Refusal to Accept

Clemente refused to accept the racial discrimination still prevalent in the American South, specifically in Florida, where the Pirates conducted spring training. Sometimes, when the team bus would stop at a restaurant that refused to serve blacks or dark-skinned Hispanics, white teammates would offer to bring food to them. Clemente told his black teammates that if they ever accepted anything brought to them from these restaurants, they would have to fight him first. The Pirates soon saw to it that black players got better treatment.

Dark-skinned Hispanics, Clemente said, were actually worse off than American blacks. "They are subjected to prejudices and stamped with generalizations," he said. "Because they speak Spanish among themselves, they are set off as a minority within a minority, and they bear the brunt of the sport's remaining prejudices." [77]

As a result, he thought, Hispanic players—himself included—seldom got the recognition they deserved. "We have self-satisfaction, yes," he said. "But after the season is over, nobody cares about us. . . . I am an American citizen. I live not so far from Miami. But some people think I live in the jungle someplace. To the people here, we are outsiders, foreigners."[78]

Clemente might have been gaining a reputation as an activist, but his search for personal recognition still had some distance to go, despite a season in which he raised his batting average to .320, second-best in the National League. He also won his third straight Gold Glove award as the best defensive right fielder.

Leader Wanted

The Pirates wanted Clemente to be something more than a stand-out player. In January 1964 Brown traveled to Puerto Rico for a four-hour meeting with his star. "Clemente can do so much more for the Pirates," Brown said later. "He could be our leader, the man we need to show the way."[79] Brown wanted Clemente to adopt the role formerly held by Long, someone who would give his fellow players encouragement or reprimands as needed, who would defuse arguments and keep peace in the locker room.

At first, Clemente declined the new role. "How can I be more of a team leader than I am?" he said in an interview. "I talk to everyone when they have a good day or a bad day. I try to help everyone out there. What more can I do?"[80]

One stumbling block to a leadership role for Clemente was his ongoing feud with Murtaugh. A team leader is supposed to be able to carry players' concerns to management and to discuss problems openly. Such a relationship between Clemente and Murtaugh, however, was unlikely. Two things occurred after the 1964 season—one in which Clemente led the major leagues with a .339 batting average—that would make leadership possible.

The first development was that Clemente was now enjoying a more stable life as a family man, having married Vera Zabala, whom he had met the previous winter. He had seen her in a San Juan pharmacy, discovered her name, and promptly called her to invite her to lunch, forgetting that custom decreed a proper introduction be made first.

Vera's Influence

One of the primary factors behind the maturing of Roberto Clemente as a person during the mid-1960s was the calming influence of his wife, Vera. Sometimes, however, Clemente was not calm, and Vera had to smooth things over.

A Pirates public relations official, Sally O'Leary, recalled a time when Clemente was signing autographs at a function in a Pittsburgh church. The line was long, and Clemente was growing impatient. Finally a small boy came forward. As he was getting his autograph, several members of his family took flash pictures.

"Roberto stopped and he looked at the people, and he said, 'Don't do that again. The flash bothers my eyes.'

"Pretty soon, Vera Clemente came up to his mother and dad and to [the boy] and she took them back to the kitchen of this church. She said, 'Can I get you some coffee and some cake? I just wanted to apologize for my husband's behavior out there. He gets a little uptight at times and he doesn't mean it. Sometimes he just goes off and says something he doesn't mean.'

"That really impressed me about Vera."

Quoted in Bruce Markusen, *Roberto Clemente: The Great One.* Champaign, IL: Sports Publishing, 1998, p. 129.

Newlyweds Roberto Clemente and Vera Cristina Zabala smile happily for pictures after their wedding on November 14, 1964.

First Date

Accordingly, some friends of Clemente's who were also friends of Vera's agreed to have a small party so that an introduction could be arranged. For their first date, she went with Clemente, appropriately enough, to a baseball game, but only on the condition that there be another couple present as chaperones.

The relationship deepened, and the couple were married on November 14, 1964, in a ceremony attended by more than one thousand people. Clemente and his bride set up housekeeping in a hillside villa costing $6,500, a huge sum for Puerto Rico, but one that was within Clemente's means as one of the best-paid players in baseball. In the years that followed, they would have three sons—Roberto Jr., Luis, and Enrique. Clemente's pride in his homeland was so strong that he made sure all his children were born in Puerto Rico, even if it meant that Vera had to fly home during the baseball season to have the baby.

Marriage had a settling effect on Clemente, who began to keep better control of his temper. In addition, Vera was the person on whom he depended most for companionship and advice. As one of their friends would say, "Roberto never made an important decision without consulting Vera; only she really knew what went on inside this complex man." [81]

Subtle Approach

The second important event was Murtaugh's resignation as manager prior to the 1965 season. He had been experiencing health problems that grew worse during the season in which the Pirates finished in a tie for sixth place. His replacement was Harry Walker, who was much more subtle in his approach to dealing with Clemente than Murtaugh had been. Whereas Murtaugh might order Clemente to take pregame outfield practice, Walker would urge him to do so, saying that if he did not, the other players would take notice and loaf. Walker acknowledged what Murtaugh never could: "He's high-spirited, a thoroughbred. He needs to be treated differently. But things mean a lot more to him than most people realize." [82]

Clemente responded by becoming the leader the Pirates wanted him to be. "Clemente's personality changed under Walker," said Nellie King. "He knew he was a hell of a ballplayer, and he started to open up as a person. He got respect under Walker. . . . And when you search for recognition so long, when it's suddenly there, you're freed." [83]

The new Clemente became more a part of the team. After out-of-town games he would often go out with his teammates rather than staying alone in his hotel room. He spent hours working with younger players, for example, teaching Matty Alou how to be a better hitter and showing Willie Stargell the tricks that had enabled him to become the top defensive outfielder in baseball.

"You could see him change over the past couple of years," catcher Jim Pagliaroni would say in 1967. "When he speaks in the clubhouse and on the field, everyone respects his word." [84] He kept a finger on the pulse of the team, chastising players when he thought they needed it, taking complaints to Walker when he thought them justified. "He keeps peace and harmony," said first baseman Donn Clendenon. "He's our goodwill ambassador,

Harry Walker (number 3) replaced Murtaugh as the Pirates' manager in 1965.

the intermediary between us and Harry Walker and the front office [the team's owners]."[85]

Injury Problems

On the field, the story was different, as Clemente had his problems. A torn ligament in his thigh—the result of a lawn-mowing mishap at home—and a bout with malaria brought him to spring training four weeks late and 10 pounds (4.5kg) underweight. Although he was in the Pirates lineup on opening day, he complained of weakness, and his batting average showed it. By May 21 he was hitting only about .250, and the Pirates had a record of 9–24.

In June, however, Clemente regained his health, and so did the Pirates. By the All-Star Game break, they had climbed to within a few games of first place, and Clemente had raised his batting average to .338, barely below that of league-leader Mays of San Francisco. Yet, when fans' votes for the All-Star team were counted, Henry (Hank) Aaron of Milwaukee and Johnny Callison of Chicago were ahead of Clemente.

He was deeply offended by this slight and, when listed as an All-Star team reserve player, declared he would not play at all. Walker took Clemente aside and explained how important it was that he represent the team and set an example for the younger players. Clemente relented and played in the game, another sign of his increasing maturity.

As Good as the President

From head to toes, Roberto Clemente is as good as the president of the United States. I believe that, and I think every man should believe that about himself.

— Roberto Clemente, quoted in Kal Wagenheim, *Clemente!* New York: Praeger, 1973, p. 5.

Following the All-Star Game, Clemente's batting average continued to climb, reaching .345 before falling off in September. Still, his .329 was good for a third National League title. It was not what he or Walker had hoped for, but the early season weakness had been too much to overcome. So, too, was the Pirates' slow start, but they finished in a solid third place.

Winning his third batting title, Clemente accepts the Silver Bat award from National League president Warren Giles in 1966.

Lofty Goals

Despite two straight batting titles in 1964 and 1965, Clemente had not come close to winning the league's Most Valuable Player award. Walker thought that what would help Clemente—and the team—would be if he adjusted his swing, trying to hit long fly balls for extra-base hits rather than line drives for singles. Walker set goals—25 home runs and 115 RBIs. These were numbers Clemente had never before achieved.

By the end of May, it appeared as if the plan had backfired. Clemente had only three home runs and had batted in only seventeen runs. Walker was patient. "I told him some things," he told an interviewer. "That he was our leader now . . . that he should set the example . . . that if he did he would win the MVP award." [86]

Clemente rose to the challenge, and the power hitter that Walker was hoping to develop appeared. He hit four home runs and drove in thirteen in an eleven-game span in June. Later in the summer he would have streaks of eleven and seventeen games with at least one hit.

The Pirates soon found themselves in a three-way fight with Los Angeles and San Francisco for the National League championship. Ultimately, however, neither Clemente's hitting nor his leadership could bring another league championship to Pittsburgh. In mid-September, the Pirates went into Los Angeles trailing the Dodgers by a game and a half in the standings, only to lose two straight. They finished third, only three games behind the Dodgers.

In spite of the lack of a championship, it had been Clemente's finest season. He had exceeded the goals Walker had set for him, ending the year with 29 home runs and 119 RBI's. Clearly he was a candidate for the MVP award, as Walker freely acknowledged: "There's no question about it. Clemente has been the guts of this team. If he's not the league's most valuable player, I'm nuts."[87]

Clemente intently watches the ball as he makes his 2,000th career hit in a September 1966 game.

Feats of Clay

Before the 1966 season, Pittsburgh manager Harry Walker urged Roberto Clemente to try to hit for more power—to try for more home runs instead of concentrating on line drives for singles. By mid-May, however, Clemente had only three home runs to his credit.

Part of the blame, he said, was the dirt in the batter's box at Forbes Field, the Pirates' home stadium. "For years I have been pleading with them to put in clay instead of sand," he said. "Sand make feet slip. Batters dig holes [with their spiked shoes], I come to the plate and scrape dirt loose to cover them up."

Whether or not Walker thought this was true was beside the point. The point was that Clemente thought it would make a difference. The sand was dug up, clay was put in, and over the next eleven days Clemente had six home runs while hitting for a .444 average.

Quoted in Phil Musick, *Who Was Roberto?* New York: Doubleday, 1974, p. 201.

MVP at Last

The vote by the baseball writers was very close. Dodgers pitcher Sandy Koufax actually had nine first-place votes to Clemente's eight, but Clemente piled up more second- and third-place votes. The point total from those votes brought him—at last—the honor he thought had been stolen from him six years before.

When reporters came to inform Clemente of the award in November, they found him driving a tractor on a small farm he had purchased. He stopped his work and said, with characteristic bluntness, "It's the highest honor a player can hope for, but I was expecting it. Of course, it could have gone to Koufax, but I had the best season of my career, and I was confident the sportswriters would vote for me."[88]

The MVP may have been the highest honor in Clemente's view, but it was not the final major one he would win. And, although he had played on one world championship team, there was still another in his future as his baseball career entered its final years.

Chapter 6

World Series Hero

A s the 1967 season rolled around, Clemente was thirty-two years old and had been playing baseball professionally— summer and winter—for sixteen years. Yet, at a time when most players his age were contemplating retirement, Clemente seemed as spry as ever, his usual complaints about injuries notwithstanding. In fact, the last third of his major-league career saw some of his most productive years and one of his top honors.

The winter of 1966–1967 was one of mixed emotions for Clemente. His status as a hero in Puerto Rico had never been higher. He became the fifth player in major-league history to receive a contract for more than one hundred thousand dollars per year. He rested his body, choosing not to play Winter League ball. He worked on his farm and opened a small restaurant. But there was sadness, as well. His eldest brother, Osvaldo, died of cancer, and another brother, Vicente, died only weeks later.

The 1967 season, likewise, evoked varied emotions. Clemente hit .357, the highest average he would ever post, to become only the seventh player ever to win four league titles. He also led the league in base hits with 209, hit 23 home runs, and batted in 110 runs. The Pirates, however, never challenged for the league lead and wound up in sixth place with a record of 81–81. Walker was fired in mid-season. Murtaugh, with whom Clemente had warred so often before, was brought back as Walker's replacement.

Nothing exemplified the frustrating nature of the season like the game on May 15 against Cincinnati. Clemente hit a home run in the first inning, another in the fifth, a double in the seventh, and a third home run in the ninth. He batted in all seven Pittsburgh runs, but the Reds scored eight. "It was my biggest game, but not my best game," he said. "My best game is when I drive in the winning run. I don't count this one. We lost."[89]

Another Mishap

There would be much more losing the following season, one that Clemente almost did not survive to see. Just as with the lawn-mowing injury years before, this one came as a result of domestic chores in

Plagued by accidents and chronic pain throughout his career, Clemente discusses his many injuries with reporters.

Puerto Rico. Two patios were terraced into a steep hill next to his house, one above the other. As he was climbing from the lower to the upper patio, an iron bar gave way and he tumbled 75 feet (23m) down the hill. Only a low retaining wall kept him from going off a cliff.

No bones were broken, but Clemente suffered a severe muscle tear in his right shoulder. He had to wear a brace most of the winter, and the shoulder was still weak when he reported for spring training. It was evident to everyone, when he failed to get a base hit in twenty-nine consecutive times at bat, that something was wrong, but nothing was made public until after the regular season began. Finally, at the end of May when he was hitting only .216, he told reporters about the injury.

It proved to be a frustrating season for Clemente, who failed to hit above .300 for the first time in nine years, and for the Pirates, who again finished in sixth place. For the first time, the Pittsburgh star began to speak openly of retirement. He told one writer, "Once upon a time, I never believed I could get tired of baseball. I played baseball from morning to night. But today it isn't as it once was. I just never seem to get enough rest. And if I can't play at my best all the time, why play?"[90] And later in the season he said, "I don't want to stop playing baseball, but if my shoulder aches this winter, I won't be back in baseball in 1969."[91]

Flawless

There are no flaws in Clemente's game. He hits the ball more viciously to the opposite field than anyone I've ever seen. He throws the ball accurately over 400 feet and he has few peers as a baserunner. And he is as fine a rightfielder as Willie Mays is a centerfielder, to me the supreme compliment.

— Bill Mazeroski, "My 16 Years with Roberto Clemente." *Sport*, November, 1971, p. 61.

When the season ended and he returned to Puerto Rico, he began to see things differently. Once, when a reporter asked him about retirement, he said, "How could I ever quit? I have thirteen people [members of his extended family] to support."[92] As so often happened, it was Vera who helped him make up his mind. "Never quit when you're down," she told him. "You have to give it another try. If you want to quit after another year, I won't say a word."[93]

Playing the Field

What really impressed baseball insiders about Roberto Clemente was not his hitting but his outstanding defensive play. Most experts rate him the finest right fielder in the history of the game.

Much of his success was the result of painstaking work. Whenever the Pirates played out of town, Clemente would reacquaint himself with the peculiarities of the right field wall of the opponents' stadium. Clemente's routine was to have a teammate hit fly balls to every corner of right field so that he could memorize how a ball would carom off the wall and at what speed.

He even took the weather into consideration. One rainy afternoon, he abruptly told a visiting friend, attorney Elfred Bernier, to drive him to Three Rivers Stadium. "The field will be wet tonight," he said. "I want to try a couple of things."

When they arrived at the stadium, Bernier said, "he had someone roll the ball on the ground to make it wet and then throw it against the wall so he could get practice grabbing it barehanded. For a long time he did that, and then he ran back and forth, stopping and starting."

Quoted in Phil Musick, *Who Was Roberto?* New York: Doubleday, 1974, p. 285.

Keeping Active

Clemente spent the winter getting his shoulder back in shape. He did not play Winter League baseball, but he kept active in several different ways. Never one to be idle, he tended to his farm and restaurant while pursuing several hobbies. He began collecting and painting driftwood. He collected bottles and ceramics. He bought a secondhand organ and taught himself to play well enough that some tunes at least were recognizable.

Any thoughts of retirement were left behind after he went to New York for a meeting of the Major League Players Association. "As soon as I saw the other players and started talking baseball," he said, "I knew I wanted to keep on playing."[94]

It was a rested and refreshed Clemente who showed up for spring training. He hit with power and seemed in top form until he injured his other shoulder diving to catch a foul ball. He was out of the lineup for more than a week, and the injury provided one of his most unforgettable quotes when he told reporters, "My bad shoulder feels good, and my good shoulder feels bad."[95]

At first it seemed as if the season would be a repeat of 1968, with Clemente hitting only .226 toward the end of May. He regained his old form in June, however, and over the last games hit .373. He and Cincinnati's Pete Rose engaged in a battle for the batting title that went down to the final inning of the final game when Rose beat out a bunt on his last time at bat. His .348 average was only .003 higher than Clemente's.

Overlooked Again

Yet, despite posting the second-highest batting average in the major leagues, he wound up seventh in the voting for the National League's Most Valuable Player award. Part of the reason, he always maintained, was racism on the part of the mostly white writers. "Things are changing a bit," he said, "but I still feel that we—Latin players, American Negroes—are foreign to white American writers."[96]

He might have added that Latin and African American players were equally foreign to most baseball fans. When a public poll was taken to determine baseball's most outstanding player of the 1960s, two whites—Koufax and Mantle—finished first and second. Clemente, whose batting average over the decade was .040 higher than Mantle's, was ninth. "I play as good as anybody," he said at one point during the following season, "but I am not loved. I don't need to be loved. I just wish it would happen."[97]

There was at least one point in the 1970 season, however, when the city of Pittsburgh and the island of Puerto Rico showed just how much they loved Clemente. On July 25, eight days after the Pirates moved from Forbes Field to their new Three Rivers Stadium, the team celebrated "Roberto Clemente Night" to honor their star player.

The players and their city had more than Clemente to celebrate. The Pirates had started slowly and in late June had lost two more games than they had won. By the time the new ballpark opened, however, they had put together some winning streaks and were leading the National League's Eastern Division. Clemente, likewise, had rebounded from a slow spring and was hitting a robust .350.

A Song for Roberto

When the night arrived, more than forty-three thousand fans crowded into Three Rivers Stadium, hundreds of them having come from Puerto Rico for the occasion. Included were Clemente's

Before pregame ceremonies, the smiling right fielder poses with his family on Roberto Clemente Night at Three Rivers Stadium in 1970.

parents, numerous dignitaries, a delegation of Puerto Rican military veterans, and a group of fifteen children from poor families. The children had composed a song for the occasion, "Roberto Clemente, the Pride of Puerto Rico."

Liking the Pressure

I never get nervous. I love this, in September, when you are in first or second [place], and each game mean something, and there are lots of people watching me. Who want to play when the game mean nothing?

— Roberto Clemente, quoted in Phil Musick, *Who Was Roberto?* New York: Doubleday, 1974, p. 209.

The pregame ceremony, telecast by satellite to thousands of other admirers in Puerto Rico, began with the Puerto Rican national anthem, "La Borinqueña." Then, each of Clemente's Hispanic teammates saluted him, placing a hand on his shoulder and bowing forward slightly. Speaker after speaker then went to the microphone set up on the infield to offer their congratulations to Clemente, who was sitting nearby with Vera and their three sons. They presented him with various proclamations and plaques, plus gifts ranging from a color television to a life-size wax figure of himself.

When it became time for Clemente to acknowledge all the accolades, he began in Spanish, his voice shaking with emotion. He dedicated the event to "all the mothers in Puerto Rico. I haven't the words to express my gratitude. I only ask that those watching this program be close to their parents, ask their blessing and embrace . . . and those friends who are watching or listening, shake hands, in the friendship that unites all Puerto Ricans."[98]

A few moments later, he switched to English, expressing his thanks and announcing that, as the result of a special appeal he had made through a local charitable organization, fifty-five hundred dollars was being donated to Pittsburgh Children's Hospital. He concluded, tears streaming down his cheeks, by saying, "There are things in life that mean the most to me, my family—and the fans in Pittsburgh and Puerto Rico."[99]

The beginning of the game itself, which the Pirates went on to win 11–10, did not put an end to the celebration. Hundreds of copies of the children's song had been printed, and throughout the game the Puerto Rican fans sang it from their seats in right field near Clemente, waving their large straw hats known as *pavas*. Non-Puerto Rican fans sitting nearby joined the singing, even though few understood the words.

More Festivities

The festivities continued the next day, with the Puerto Rican visitors taking in the sights. Wherever they went, the people of Pittsburgh—cab drivers, store owners, waiters—refused to let them pay as soon as they learned their guests had come from their island to honor Clemente.

After a private banquet that night, Clemente encountered the group of children. They formed a circle around him, one boy reading a poem, after which another boy played guitar and sang "Soñando con Puerto Rico," or "Dreaming of Puerto Rico." Juan

Still displaying dazzling fielding at the age of thirty-four, Clemente runs to catch a fly ball during a 1971 game.

Jiménez, a businessman who had arranged for the children's trip, recalled, "Well, I'll tell you, Clemente starts to cry, his wife starts to cry, the kids start to cry, about a hundred fifty Puerto Ricans gathered around, they all start to cry." [100]

The remainder of the season was less than festive for Clemente. Despite some good hitting streaks, he was beset by injuries that he could not shake off, even having undergone unorthodox treatments such as a pregame rubdown with goat's milk. He missed a total of fifty-four games for the season and, although his batting average was .352—second best in the league—he did not come to bat often enough to be considered for the batting championship.

Clemente missed most of September but returned to the lineup in time to help Pittsburgh win the Eastern Division championship. The Pirates' hopes for another World Series, however, evaporated when they were swept, three games to none, by the San Francisco Giants in the National League Championship Series. Clemente struggled along with most of his teammates during the three games, getting only two hits in fourteen at bats.

At Three Rivers Stadium, Clemente hugs the bag after sliding on base during the 1971 World Series against the Baltimore Orioles.

Needing His Rest

There was no question of Clemente not returning in 1971, but everyone realized that he would need periodic rests if he was to avoid the kind of injuries that were likely to sideline him for weeks. Still, however, he was the central figure on the Pirates team, not only on the field but as a leader in the locker room and as an adviser to management. Brown began asking his opinion before acquiring players from other teams in trades.

A Real Hitter

Roberto can hit any pitch, anywhere, at any time. He will hit pitchouts. He will hit brush-back pitches. He will hit high, inside pitches to the opposite field, which would be ridiculous even if he didn't do it with both feet off the ground.

— Los Angeles Dodgers pitcher Sandy Koufax, quoted in Phil Musick, *Who Was Roberto?* New York: Doubleday, 1974, p. 230.

As in recent years, Clemente started the 1971 season slowly. His batting average in April was only about .250, and he did not get his first home run until May 11. He bridled, however, when reporters suggested that he needed to retire. "They always say, 'Retire when you're on top,'" he said. "I'll quit when I should quit. No one will tell me when to quit." [101]

As the season progressed, talk of Clemente's retirement declined as his batting average increased. By mid-June he was hitting .313. He also continued to play superlative defense, despite being considered at thirty-six, old for an outfielder. Taking their cues from Clemente, the Pirates played inspired baseball throughout the season, rallying from an August slump to win their division by seven games and move on to battle San Francisco for a spot in the World Series.

The Pirates had lost four consecutive games in San Francisco's Candlestick Park, and the Giants made it five in a row, winning 5–4 to open the championship series. The Pirates came back the next day though, 9–4, to break the streak and then took two straight in Pittsburgh to advance to the World Series. In the deciding game, Clemente batted in three runs, the last one putting the Pirates ahead for good.

Clemente hits a home run in the seventh game of the World Series against Baltimore in 1971 at the Orioles' Memorial Stadium.

The Orioles

Pittsburgh's World Series opponents would be the Baltimore Orioles, who were listed as heavy favorites by the experts. The Orioles had four pitchers who had won twenty or more games that season and offensive stars like Frank Robinson and Brooks Robinson. They had won the American League East by twelve games and swept the Oakland Athletics in the championship series.

The World Series opened in Baltimore, and Clemente, despite a case of food poisoning the night before the opener, got two hits in each of the first two games. It was not enough, though, as Baltimore won 5–3 and 11–3. The experts began saying the Pirates would lose four straight, and one columnist wrote, "The World Series is no longer a contest; it's an atrocity."[102]

But the Pittsburgh team that had rallied in August now did the same in October. With Clemente getting his fifth base hit of the series, the Pirates won game three, 5–1. After the game, New York columnist Dick Young wrote, "The best damn ballplayer in the World Series, maybe in the whole world, is Roberto Clemente. . . . Maybe some guys hit the ball farther, and some throw it harder, and one or two run faster, though I doubt that, but nobody puts it all together like Roberto."[103]

Clemente had much more to show the national media. In the fourth game, the first in World Series history to be played at night, he collected three more hits as the Pirates won, 4–3. He got one more the next day and knocked in a run as Pittsburgh won, 4–0, to take a three-games-to-two lead.

Back to Baltimore

The series moved back to Baltimore for the sixth game, and Clemente continued his hitting streak. He hit a triple in the first inning and a home run in the third, but the Orioles won, 3–2. Just as in 1960, when the Pirates had last played in the World Series, everything would be riding on one game.

In the locker room before the next day's deciding game, Clemente encountered Haak, the scout who had convinced him not to quit in mid-season seventeen years earlier in Montreal. "Howie, you have been a good friend of mine over the years," he said. "I want you to be one of the first to know something. If we win today's game, I'm going to quit baseball."[104]

Pittsburgh pitcher Steve Blass held Baltimore scoreless through four innings, but the Orioles' Mike Cuellar was even more effective, retiring eleven batters in a row before Clemente came to bat with two outs in the fourth inning. Cuellar's first pitch was a curve ball, and Clemente—who usually never swung at a first pitch—unleashed a long drive to left-center field. Two Baltimore outfielders drifted back, thinking they could make a play, but the ball carried into the stands for a home run. Clemente had given his team a lead they would never lose, eventually wining 2–1 to become world champions.

When the game ended, Clemente joined his teammates for a midfield celebration, then headed for the locker room, thinking he had played his final game. Before he got there, however, he saw Vera sitting behind the Pirates' dugout. "She said, 'Don't quit now. Baseball's your life,'" Clemente said later. "She was crying. I changed my mind."[105] Clemente had decided to return for the 1972 season, but neither he, Vera, nor anyone else could have known it was to be his last.

Chapter 7

Last Innings

The 1971 World Series brought Clemente the widespread acclaim he had long—undeservedly, he thought—been denied. His national recognition, and his immeasurable status in Puerto Rico, gave him a foundation from which to expand his attacks on racism, his encouragement of fellow Hispanic players, and his widening efforts on behalf of humanity. This would also be the year Clemente reached one of baseball's most cherished milestones.

After the World Series, sportswriters who had long ignored him now paid tribute. "Roberto Clemente is discovered every 10 or 11 years, when the Bucs make it to the World Series," a New York writer conceded. "That is when he gets the ink he should have been getting the rest of the time."[106]

Clemente was honored at banquets in Pittsburgh and New York City, but the accolades he received there were slight compared to the adoration heaped on him in Puerto Rico. Thousands of fans met his plane in San Juan on his return, and dozens of cars followed Clemente and his wife along the road to their home, their horns honking.

He did not play Winter League ball in 1971–1972. He did not have the time. Friends, relatives, and total strangers—even tourists—came to his house at all hours. He and Vera had hoped to spend much of the winter in a small home they had bought high in the hills, but they got there only on three occasions.

In Demand

Rarely did Clemente turn down a request for an appearance. "I had so many things going on down there [San Juan], and I just

Always happy to accommodate his fans, Clemente talks to a young boy about batting techniques in Pittsburgh in 1961.

couldn't say no," he said. "Every day I was doing something different."[107]

What he was doing, however, was merely an extension of what he had always done—giving freely of his time and money to various causes. He was well aware of his status as a role model for Puerto Rican youth and took it very seriously. "A country without idols is nothing,"[108] he said. He knew his limitations, however, and politely declined when some leading citizens of San Juan asked him to run for mayor.

Clemente was especially interested in trying to help children, with whom he seemed to relate better than most adults. Throughout his career he had staged baseball clinics for children from low-income families, showing them how to play but emphasizing that success came only with hard work.

He was deeply concerned about the dangers of drug abuse and at one point brought a nephew with drug problems to live with him in Pittsburgh where he could keep an eye on him. On one occasion he agreed to do a television announcement warning teenagers about drugs, but only on the condition that a second version be done in Spanish. When the producer asked who would translate the English script, Clemente said he would and spent almost an hour doing so before filming began.

A Historic Lineup

On September 1, 1972, Roberto Clemente became one-ninth of baseball history. The event came about because of injuries to two Pirates regulars, first baseman Bob Robertson and third baseman Richie Hebner.

Manager Danny Murtaugh had to make substitutions for his ailing players, and his lineup consisted of Rennie Stennett at second base, Gene Clines in center field, Clemente in right field, Willie Stargell in left field, Emanuel "Manny" Sanguillen catching, Dave Cash at third base, Al Oliver at first base, Jackie Hernandez at shortstop, and Dock Ellis pitching.

Research subsequently showed that this was the first all-black, all-Hispanic starting lineup in the history of Major League Baseball. Clemente had two base hits as the Pirates defeated Philadelphia, 10–7.

Giving Advice

In addition to serving as a role model, Clemente actively counseled young baseball players from throughout Latin America. Arturo Garcia, a chiropractor who treated him over the years, later recalled him saying, "I don't care if they're Puerto Rican or not; they can be Dominican, Venezuelan, Cuban, Mexican, they're *Latinos,* my people."[109]

Clemente well remembered that his first contract from a major-league team could have been much larger had he received better advice. He warned up-and-coming Hispanic players against falling into the same trap. "I don't think they are going to offer you the money you are worth," he told future major leaguer Willie Montañez. "You can get more if you wait, or maybe talk to other teams. Don't make the mistake of settling for less than you're worth."[110]

The success of Clemente and other stars in the 1950s and 1960s opened the eyes of young Hispanics to their potential and opened the eyes of others, as well. "They pointed the way to Latin America," said Marcos Breton. "I've heard more than one Latin scout say that an American general manager . . . will tell them, 'Find me a Clemente.' That's an awful tall order. But maybe in the process of looking for that ideal, they find an awful lot of talent along the way."[111]

Speaking Out

Clemente continued to speak out against what he considered the second-class status accorded blacks and Hispanics by the mostly Anglo baseball establishment in the United States. "My greatest satisfaction comes from helping to erase the old opinion about Latin Americans and blacks," he said. "People never questioned our ability, but they considered us inferior to their station in life. . . . I don't blame the fans for that. I blame the writers. They made it look like we were entirely different from white players."[112]

Many of Clemente's off-the-field deeds were done quietly, since he neither wanted nor sought publicity. Many stories relate how he would help people, often strangers, in need. Such aid could be financial, but often it was simply in the form of an act of kindness.

Early in Clemente's career with the Pirates, for instance, a wheel-chair-bound young fan and her mother missed a bus home from a game because they were waiting for his autograph. Clemente took them on the 30-mile (48km) trip in his own car.

His concern for his own body led to concern about the health of others. He learned so much about the the nature of the human back and back injuries that he began treating others on an informal basis. Elderly men and women, bent over from years of physical labor, would sometimes come unannounced to his home, and he would manipulate their muscles and spines until they felt better.

Back to Baseball

Finally, however, the whirlwind winter was over and it was time to return to Florida for spring training. Even with all that Clemente had accomplished, there was one goal plainly in sight—his 3,000th base hit. Only ten men had ever reached that plateau, and the list, while it included such legends as Ty Cobb, Musial, Mays, and Aaron, contained no Hispanics.

A few years earlier, during one of his injury-plagued spells, Clemente had doubted his chances of making it to 3,000. Going into the 1972 season, however, he found himself just 118 hits short of this milestone. Publicly, he said reaching 3,000 did not mean much to him. Privately, he felt otherwise. He told his good friend and teammate Manny Sanguillen, "Sangy, I've *got* to get those 3,000 hits. I might get sick or die, and no other Latin will do it."[113]

Although his batting eye seemed as accurate as ever, it appeared that injuries and illness might prevent him from reaching the goal. While he was hitting well over .300 by August, he had missed 47 of the Pirates' first 116 games. He went into September still needing 25 hits with only 26 games remaining.

Suddenly, however, his health improved and the hits began coming. On September 28 in Philadelphia, during the Pirates' next-to-last series, he got number 2,999 and immediately asked to be taken out of the game. He wanted to hit number 3,000 back home in Pittsburgh, where the Pirates would face the New York Mets.

At bat against New York Mets pitcher Jon Matlack, Clemente connects bat with ball for his 3,000th hit on September 30, 1972.

Close, But Not Quite

In his first time at bat against New York, Clemente hit a soft ground ball up the middle that eluded pitcher Tom Seaver. Mets short-stop Ken Boswell charged hard, but the ball skipped off his glove. Clemente reached first base safely, but the official scorer ruled the play an error on Boswell rather than a hit by Clemente, who went hitless the rest of the night.

The next afternoon, leading off the fourth inning against pitch-er Jon Matlack, Clemente let the first pitch go by for a strike. The next pitch was a curve ball that failed to break down over the plate, instead staying high in the strike zone. It was a tempting target, and Clemente took full advantage, lashing it against the center-field wall for a double.

The crowd roared its approval and kept up its applause for sev-eral minutes, delaying the game. The ball was retrieved and given to Clemente as a souvenir. After the inning, Willie Mays, now in the last stage of his career, came over from the Mets' dugout to shake Clemente's hand.

His 3,000th hit safely in the record books, Clemente was replaced in right field and sat out most of the Pirates' final four regular season games. He had played in 102 games, the fewest in his major-league career, but had a batting average of .312 and had completed his first-ever season without committing a single error.

Still more baseball remained, however, since Pittsburgh had won the National League East and was to meet Cincinnati to play for a spot in the World Series. It turned out to be a disappointing end to the season both for the Pirates and Clemente. Cincinnati won the championship series, three games to two, with Clemente hitting only .214. After the final game, Clemente spoke to his teammates in their somber locker room. "Pick up your head," he shouted. "We don't quit now. We go home and come back in February [for spring training]."[114] They were words the Pirates would remember.

A Wounded Heart

Roberto's death has left such a deep wound in my heart. Wherever I am, working. Sitting. It's so painful. . . . I've always said, 'God's will be done,' but let him give me a sign of Roberto! We never saw him get into the plane. He just disappeared. Not a single sign.

— Luisa Walker de Clemente, Roberto's mother, quoted in Kal Wagenheim, *Clemente!* New York: Praeger, 1973, p. 16.

Back in Puerto Rico, Clemente resumed his crowded schedule of work on civic projects and personal pursuits. He once again decided against playing in the Winter League, but he agreed to manage a Puerto Rican team during an amateur tournament in Nicaragua. He spent almost a month there, and, according to Luis Mayoral, "kind of fell in love with the people of Nicaragua."[115]

The Earthquake

It was natural, then, that when a massive earthquake struck Nicaragua on December 23, destroying much of the capital city of Managua, Clemente sought to help. He went on television to urge the people of Puerto Rico to donate money and relief supplies to be sent to Nicaragua.

The fateful plane carrying Clemente and four others to their deaths on December 31, 1972, was similar to this DC-7 model.

Clemente was honorary chairman of the relief committee, but he treated it as anything but an honorary position. He appeared frequently on radio and television, made personal appearances at locales where supplies were being collected, and even went door-to-door in wealthy neighborhoods asking for donations.

Clemente arranged to lease an airplane to deliver the supplies and then, when the plane proved too small to transport what had been gathered, hired a ship. Then, shortly after Christmas, the Nicaraguan government sent out an urgent plea for medical supplies. In response, Clemente made arrangements for a second plane, this one an aging DC-7, a four-engine turboprop with more cargo room than the first.

Clemente had wanted to fly to Nicaragua to supervise relief efforts in person but had been convinced to stay in Puerto Rico to raise more money. Now, however, he heard a report that corrupt elements of the Nicaraguan army were intercepting some supplies intended for earthquake victims. He felt he had to go to put a stop to such diversions.

A Fatal Error

After the plane crash that claimed the life of Roberto Clemente and four other men, investigators tried to piece together what had gone wrong. Their best clue was the fact that divers found the plane's landing gear lowered and locked and the wing flaps raised.

While it was never proved, the most plausible theory was that, after an engine failed on takeoff, pilot Jerry Hill ordered copilot Arturo Rivera, president of the company that owned the DC-7, to raise the landing gear to reduce the drag on the plane. Rivera, it is thought, mistakenly raised the flaps. The combination of the raised flaps and lowered landing gear might have caused the plane to abruptly dive into the ocean.

Rivera, in fact, had been repeatedly cited by the Federal Aviation Administration (FAA) for conducting unsafe and unlicensed flights, and the FAA had recommended his pilot's license be permanently revoked. The National Transportation Safety Board had reduced the ban to a suspension of 180 days. Rivera had gotten his license back just six months before the fatal flight.

The flight in the DC-7 was scheduled for December 30, but there were problems. The twenty-year-old plane, which had not been flown in four months, had been shipped to the San Juan airport. Shortly before the flight, as the plane was being moved from a hangar, two propellers were damaged and had to be replaced.

Finding a Crew

In addition to the mechanical problems, the approach of New Year's made it hard to find a crew. Finally, a retired Air Force pilot, Jerry Hill, volunteered. The plane's owner, Arturo Rivera, agreed to be the copilot when no one else could be found. A local airplane mechanic, Francisco Mathías, was recruited as flight engineer. The passengers were Clemente and a friend, Angel Lozano.

Vera drove her husband to the airport, leaving their children with her mother. The grandmother later said that young Robertito told her, "Grandma, grandma, *papi* is going to Nicaragua, and he won't be back."[116]

Others were equally disturbed. Pirate teammate José Pagan, who had gone to the airport, thought the DC-7 looked overloaded. "Don't do it," he advised Clemente. "You know everything about baseball, but very little about airplanes."[117] Clemente, however, would not be dissuaded. The plane was supposed to leave at 4:00 P.M., but there were some last-minute mechanical difficulties. Vera and the others decided not to wait and returned home.

Actually, it was not until shortly after 9:00 P.M. that the plane taxied down the runway and became airborne. One airport employee later reported seeing fire on the left wing. A moment later, as Hill radioed that he was turning back toward the airport, the plane vanished from the control tower radar screen.

A man living about 1 mile (1.6km) from the airport, José Paris, saw the plane flying low over the water. There was a series of explosions, and the DC-7 nosedived into the sea about a mile (1.6km) from shore. Within five minutes there was no trace left on the surface.

Getting the News

Shortly after midnight, Vera received a phone call from a niece saying the plane had crashed. She sped to the airport. Flares lit the area of the ocean where the plane had gone down. Boats searched the surface but found nothing. The next day—New Year's Day 1973—Vera waited on the shore with thousands of others as the U.S. Coast Guard continued the search in vain.

A Great Person

He was one of the greatest persons I knew. If you have to die, how better could your death be exemplified than by being on a mission of mercy?

— Pittsburgh Pirates Chairman of the Board of Directors John Galbreath, quoted in Arnold Hano, *Roberto Clemente: Batting King*. New York: G.P. Putnam's Sons, 1973, p. 186.

Four days after the crash, a memorial service was conducted in Clemente's hometown of Carolina. The mourners from Puerto Rico were joined by hundreds from the United States, including all the Pittsburgh Pirates players and their wives. Pitcher Steve Blass delivered a eulogy including a poem that ended

> Let this be a silent token
> Of lasting friendship's gleam.
> And all that we've left unspoken—
> Your friends on the Pirate team.[118]

Virtually the entire island of Puerto Rico went into a state of mourning. "The passing of Clemente was like the death of God,"[119] one observer said. Pittsburgh, too, felt a tremendous loss. Thousands attended memorial services, and high on a hill overlooking downtown, a neon advertising sign was changed to read ADIOS, AMIGO.

In a 1973 ceremony, Pittsburgh Pirates chairman John Galbreath presents a uniform bearing Clemente's now-retired number 21 to his mother Luisa Clemente.

Hall of Fame

Almost immediately, fans began calling for a special election to put Clemente into the Baseball Hall of Fame. Newspapers quickly took up the cause. The problem was that the rules mandated that a player be retired for five years before becoming eligible for election. On January 3 the Baseball Writers of America announced that the rule would be waived in Clemente's case and a special election held.

A Man of the People

In Puerto Rico, the people still love him, and he's a big man; they never forget him. Every time it's a special anniversary, they commemorate it on radio and TV. He's still on everyone's mind.

— Vera Clemente, quoted in Jim O'Brien, *Remember Roberto*. Pittsburgh, Geyer, 1994, p. 53.

Clemente had once visited the Hall of Fame in Cooperstown, New York, and been told by a fan that he would one day be a member. Reflecting on his often strained relations with the media, Clemente said, ironically as it turned out, "I guess a fellow like me has to die to get voted in by the writers."[120]

When the ballots were counted, Clemente received favorable votes from all but 31 of the 424 electors. Moreover, many who had voted "no" explained that they were not against Clemente, only opposed to the waiving of the five-year rule.

On August 6, the baseball world gathered in Cooperstown for Clemente's induction into the Hall of Fame, the first Hispanic to be so honored. Vera was there, along with her three sons and Roberto's mother. When Vera's turn to speak came, she said, "This is a momentous last triumph, and if he were here, he would dedicate it to our people of Puerto Rico, our people in Pittsburgh, and to all his fans throughout the United States."[121]

Of all the tributes to Clemente, however, perhaps the most eloquent was by Baseball Commissioner Bowie Kuhn: "He gave the term 'complete' a new meaning. He was a man of fierce pride and deep compassion for his fellow man. He was indeed the perfect and classic ballplayer. He made the word 'superstar' seem inadequate. He had about him a touch of royalty. Somehow, somewhere, for me, he should have been a king."[122]

Epilogue

Ciudad Deportiva

E lection to the Hall of Fame was the greatest honor Clemente could have received, but it was far from being the only one. Eventually two hospitals, more than thirty schools, and a bridge in Pittsburgh would bear his name. But the legacy that he probably would have treasured most is *Ciudad Deportiva*, "Sports City."

As early as 1959 Clemente had told friends of his desire to establish a place where children could learn not only baseball and other sports, but also the value of teamwork and pride in their accomplishments. "This is my dream," he said. "I do not know exactly what sports city will be like . . . but it will be beautiful. It will be open to everybody. No matter who they are. . . . I will do this thing because this is what God meant me to do. Baseball is just something that gave me a chance to do this." [123]

Clemente's fame after the 1971 World Series got the project moving, but it was only after his death that the government of Puerto Rico and private donors stepped forward to make Clemente's dream a reality. Fans in both Puerto Rico and the United States donated more than five hundred thousand dollars. The government donated the land, a former naval base near Clemente's hometown of Carolina. Some facilities—two baseball diamonds and a swimming pool—were already in place, and the complex opened in 1974. Much of the rest of the land was swampy, however, and it took more than ten years before expansion began.

Today, however, *Ciudad Deportiva* boasts a gymnasium with four basketball/volleyball courts and four tennis courts, a track-and-field center, six baseball fields, and a large open area that can serve either for soccer or football. More than two hundred thousand young people, not only from Puerto Rico but from throughout Latin America, come to Sports City each year to take part in the programs offered there. The emphasis is on sports, but the over-riding purpose, according to Spanish-language baseball broadcaster Marcos Breton after visiting the facility, is "in trying to build

A Question of Dignity

Roberto Clemente was an intensely proud man. He was quick to take offense if he thought anyone was trying to take advantage of him—even if they were giving him a valuable gift. Bob Leith, a Puerto Rican businessman who owned the San Juan Winter League team when Clemente was a player, remembered such an occasion.

After the 1971 World Series, in which Clemente was named Most Valuable Player, a large group of Puerto Rican fans pooled their contributions to buy him a new Cadillac automobile. The problem was that there was no Cadillac dealership in Puerto Rico, so the car had to be purchased in the United States and shipped to the island.

"When it reached Puerto Rico," said Leith, "Roberto had to pay an excise tax of $5,250 to get it on the island. . . . Well, that really hurt Roberto. 'How come I gotta pay for a gift?' he asks me. 'Roberto, you're like anybody else, you've got to pay the tax, gift or not.'"

Leith finally went to Puerto Rican government officials, who agreed to pay Clemente the $5,250 to give a series of speeches in the United States on behalf of Puerto Rican tourism. He would then use that money to pay the tax.

"The funny thing is," said Leith, "he made the speeches, but he never sent the bill to the government to get his money back. The mere fact that he thought he could get it was enough. It was a question of *dignidad*. I don't think that people in the states quite put the value on dignity that he and a lot of other people do."

Quoted in Kal Wagenheim, *Clemente!* New York: Praeger, 1973, p. 187.

good citizens. They [Vera Clemente and her family] want children there to be good people and good citizens above everything else."[124]

Of the millions of young people who have taken advantage of Sports City, a few have followed Clemente's path to baseball fame. Others will surely come after, following their dreams up the long driveway past the statue of Clemente. As they pass by, the statue seems to speak Clemente's words from years before: "Anytime you have the opportunity to accomplish something for somebody who comes behind you and you don't do it, you are wasting your time on this earth."[125]

Notes

Introduction: *"El día más grande"*
1. Quoted in Bruce Markusen, *Roberto Clemente: The Great One.* Champaign, IL: Sports Publishing, 1998, p. 278.
2. Quoted in Markusen, *Roberto Clemente,* p. 278.
3. Quoted in Phil Musick, *Who Was Roberto?* New York: Doubleday, 1974, p. 278.
4. Quoted in Jim O'Brien, *Remember Roberto.* Pittsburgh: Geyer, 1994, p. 316.
5. Quoted in Arnold Hano, *Roberto Clemente: Batting King.* New York: G.P. Putnam's Sons, 1973, p. 182.
6. Quoted in Hano, *Roberto Clemente,* p. 183.

Chapter One: "God Wished It"
7. Quoted in Markusen, *Roberto Clemente,* p. 4.
8. Quoted in Hano, *Roberto Clemente,* p. 20.
9. Quoted in Musick, *Who Was Roberto?* p. 53.
10. Quoted in Musick, *Who Was Roberto?* p. 52.
11. Quoted in Markusen, *Roberto Clemente,* p. 3.
12. Quoted in Kal Wagenheim, *Clemente!* New York: Praeger, 1973, p. 22.
13. Quoted in Markusen, *Roberto Clemente,* p. 3.
14. Quoted in Musick, *Who Was Roberto?* p. 57.
15. Quoted in Musick, *Who Was Roberto?* p. 62.
16. Quoted in Musick, *Who Was Roberto?* p. 64.
17. Quoted in Wagenheim, *Clemente!* p. 31.
18. Quoted in Markusen, *Roberto Clemente,* p. 11.
19. Quoted in Wagenheim, *Clemente!* p. 24.
20. Quoted in Wagenheim, *Clemente!* p. 25.
21. Quoted in Musick, *Who Was Roberto?* p. 72.
22. Quoted in Musick, *Who Was Roberto?* p. 74.
23. Quoted in Musick, *Who Was Roberto?* p. 74.
24. Quoted in Wagenheim, *Clemente!* p. 34.

Chapter Two: Hidden and Discovered

25. Quoted in Musick, *Who Was Roberto?* p. 78.
26. Quoted in Musick, *Who Was Roberto?* p. 81.
27. Quoted in Markusen, *Roberto Clemente,* p. 19.
28. Quoted in Wagenheim, *Clemente!* p. 40.
29. Quoted in Hano, *Roberto Clemente,* p. 28.
30. Quoted in Hano, *Roberto Clemente,* p. 28.
31. Quoted in Wagenheim, *Clemente!* p. 42.
32. Quoted in Musick, *Who Was Roberto?* p. 86.
33. Quoted in Bill Christine, *Roberto.* New York: Stadia Sports, 1973, p. 61.
34. Quoted in Christine, *Roberto,* p. 62.
35. Quoted in Markusen, *Roberto Clemente,* p. 29.
36. Quoted in Wagenheim, *Clemente!* p. 42.

Chapter Three: Learning Curve

37. Quoted in Markusen, *Roberto Clemente,* p. 39.
38. Quoted in Wagenheim, *Clemente!* p. 53.
39. Quoted in Markusen, *Roberto Clemente,* p. 38.
40. Quoted in Markusen, *Roberto Clemente,* p. 37.
41. Quoted in Markusen, *Roberto Clemente,* p. 74.
42. Quoted in Hano, *Roberto Clemente,* p. 44.
43. Quoted in Wagenheim, *Clemente!* p. 57.
44. Quoted in Markusen, *Roberto Clemente,* p. 59.
45. Quoted in Wagenheim, *Clemente!* p. 69.
46. Quoted in Wagenheim, *Clemente!* p. 69.
47. Quoted in Musick, *Who Was Roberto?* p. 137.
48. Quoted in Markusen, *Roberto Clemente,* p. 63.
49. Quoted in Wagenheim, *Clemente!* p. 71.
50. Quoted in Markusen, *Roberto Clemente,* p. 65.
51. Quoted in Musick, *Who Was Roberto?* p. 143.
52. Quoted in Markusen, *Roberto Clemente,* p. 67.
53. Quoted in Wagenheim, *Clemente!* p. 72.

Chapter Four: The Making of a Superstar

54. Quoted in Markusen, *Roberto Clemente,* p. 80.
55. Quoted in Stew Thornley, "Roberto Clemente," The Baseball Biography Project. http://bioproj.sabr.org/bioproj.cfm?a=v&v=l&bid=1255&pid=2553.

56. Quoted in Markusen, *Roberto Clemente,* p. 80.
57. Quoted in Wagenheim, *Clemente!* p. 75.
58. Quoted in Wagenheim, *Clemente!* p. 73.
59. Quoted in Wagenheim, *Clemente!* p. 74.
60. Quoted in Musick, *Who Was Roberto?* p. 148.
61. Bill Mazeroski, "My 16 Years with Roberto Clemente." *Sport,* November 1971, p. 61.
62. Quoted in Musick, *Who Was Roberto?* p. 149.
63. Quoted in Hano, *Roberto Clemente,* p. 110.
64. Quoted in Wagenheim, *Clemente!* p. 85.
65. Quoted in Markusen, *Roberto Clemente,* p. 102.
66. Quoted in Markusen, *Roberto Clemente,* p. 102.
67. Quoted in Musick, *Who Was Roberto?* p. 153.
68. Quoted in Wagenheim, *Clemente!* p. 92.
69. Quoted in Markusen, *Roberto Clemente,* p. 104.

Chapter Five: The Road to the MVP

70. Quoted in Hano, *Roberto Clemente,* p. 143.
71. Quoted in Wagenheim, *Clemente!* p. 103.
72. Quoted in Wagenheim, *Clemente!* p. 104.
73. Quoted in Musick, *Who Was Roberto?* p. 167.
74. Quoted in Markusen, *Roberto Clemente,* p. 124.
75. Quoted in Christine, *Roberto,* p. 74.
76. Quoted in Hano, *Roberto Clemente,* p. 135.
77. Quoted in Wagenheim, *Clemente!* p. 99.
78. Quoted in Wagenheim, *Clemente!* p. 129.
79. Quoted in Markusen, *Roberto Clemente,* p. 122.
80. Quoted in Wagenheim, *Clemente!* p. 120.
81. Quoted in Wagenheim, *Clemente!* p. 102.
82. Quoted in Musick, *Who Was Roberto?* p. 197.
83. Quoted in Musick, *Who Was Roberto?* p. 196.
84. Quoted in Wagenheim, *Clemente!* p. 133.
85. Quoted in Wagenheim, *Clemente!* p. 132.
86. Quoted in Musick, *Who Was Roberto?* p. 199.
87. Quoted in Wagenheim, *Clemente!* p. 130.
88. Quoted in Hano, *Roberto Clemente,* p. 173.

Chapter Six: World Series Hero

89. Quoted in Wagenheim, *Clemente!* p. 134.
90. Quoted in Markusen, *Roberto Clemente,* p. 167.

91. Quoted in Musick, *Who Was Roberto?* p. 238.
92. Quoted in Musick, *Who Was Roberto?* p. 238.
93. Quoted in Wagenheim, *Clemente!* p. 149.
94. Quoted in Wagenheim, *Clemente!* p. 150.
95. Quoted in Markusen, *Roberto Clemente,* p. 181.
96. Quoted in Wagenheim, *Clemente!* p. 157.
97. Quoted in Musick, *Who Was Roberto?* p. 256.
98. Quoted in Wagenheim, *Clemente!* p. 181.
99. Quoted in Markusen, *Roberto Clemente,* p. 195.
100. Quoted in Wagenheim, *Clemente!* p. 186.
101. Quoted in Markusen, *Roberto Clemente,* p. 217.
102. Quoted in Wagenheim, *Clemente!* p. 197.
103. Quoted in Markusen, *Roberto Clemente,* p. 259.
104. Quoted in Markusen, *Roberto Clemente,* p. 271.
105. Quoted in Musick, *Who Was Roberto?* p. 278.

Chapter Seven: Last Innings

106. Quoted in Markusen, *Roberto Clemente,* p. 280.
107. Quoted in Musick, *Who Was Roberto?* p. 283.
108. Quoted in Musick, *Who Was Roberto?* p. 305.
109. Quoted in Wagenheim, *Clemente!* p. 117.
110. Quoted in Wagenheim, *Clemente!* p. 107.
111. Quoted in Markusen, *Roberto Clemente,* p. 350.
112. Quoted in Wagenheim, *Clemente!* p. 215.
113. Quoted in Wagenheim, *Clemente!* p. 220.
114. Quoted in Markusen, *Roberto Clemente,* p. 303.
115. Quoted in Markusen, *Roberto Clemente,* p. 311.
116. Quoted in Wagenheim, *Clemente!* p. 244.
117. Quoted in Markusen, *Roberto Clemente,* p. 313.
118. Quoted in Markusen, *Roberto Clemente,* p. 323.
119. Quoted in Musick, *Who Was Roberto?* p. 43.
120. Quoted in Markusen, *Roberto Clemente,* p. 325.
121. Quoted in Markusen, *Roberto Clemente,* p. 327.
122. Quoted in Musick, *Who Was Roberto?* p. 303.

Epilogue: *Ciudad Deportiva*

123. Quoted in Musick, *Who Was Roberto?* p. 305.
124. Quoted in Markusen, *Roberto Clemente,* p. 348.
125. Quoted in Musick, *Who Was Roberto?* p. 234.

Important Dates

August 18, 1934
Born in Carolina, Puerto Rico.

October 9, 1952
Signed to first professional baseball contract by Santurce of Puerto Rican Winter League.

February 19, 1954
Signed to minor-league contract by Brooklyn Dodgers.

November 22, 1954
Taken in baseball draft by Pittsburgh Pirates.

April 17, 1955
Singles in first at bat as a major league player.

September 1961
Wins first of four National League batting championships; wins first of twelve Gold Glove awards as top defensive right fielder.

November 14, 1964
Marries Vera Cristina Zabala.

September 2, 1966
Records 2,000th base hit.

November 16, 1966
Named National League's Most Valuable Player for 1966 season.

July 25, 1970
Honored at Roberto Clemente Night in Pittsburgh.

October 17, 1971
Named Most Valuable Player of 1971 World Series.

September 30, 1972
Becomes eleventh player in major league history to reach three thousand base hits.

December 31, 1972
Killed in airplane crash off the coast of Puerto Rico.

August 6, 1973
Becomes first Hispanic player inducted into the Baseball Hall of Fame.

For More Information

Books

Peter C. Bjarkman, *Baseball with a Latin Beat: A History of the Latin American Game*. Jefferson, NC: McFarland, 1994. Thorough and very interesting history of baseball in Latin America from its introduction after the Spanish-American War.

Carin T. Ford, *Roberto Clemente, Baseball Legend*. Berkeley Heights, NJ: Enslow, 2005. Part of the Latino Biography Library series, this account of Clemente's life is well told and supplemented by full-color pictures.

Wil Mara, *Roberto Clemente*. New York: Children's Press, 2005. Written for younger readers, this biography tells the story of Clemente in easy-to-read language.

Bruce Markusen, *The Team that Changed Baseball: Roberto Clemente and the 1971 Pittsburgh Pirates*. Yardley, PA: Westholme, 2006. Story of Major League Baseball's first truly integrated team and how it won the World Series.

Heron Marquez, *Roberto Clemente: Baseball's Humanitarian Hero*. Minneapolis: Carolrhoda, 2004. Well-written and illustrated account of Clemente's life and career.

Fred McMane, *The 3,000 Hit Club*. Champaign, IL: Sports Publishing, 2000. Short biographies of all Major League Baseball players to have reached the three thousand-hit milestone. Roberto Clemente was the eleventh player to do so, and there have been thirteen more added to the list up to the date of publication.

Jim O'Brien, *Remember Roberto*. Pittsburgh: Geyer, 1994. Dozens of short, first-hand accounts of people who knew Clemente, including family members, friends, teammates, and sportswriters.

Paul Robert Walker, *Pride of Puerto Rico: The Life of Roberto Clemente*. San Diego: Harcourt Brace Jovanovich, 1998. Part biography, part fiction, this account of Clemente's life blends biographical information with fictionalized dialog, especially in telling about Clemente's childhood.

Jonah Winter, *Roberto Clemente: Pride of the Pittsburgh Pirates.* New York: Atheneum, 2005. Also designed for younger readers, this well-reviewed book on Clemente's life features illustrations by Raul Colon.

Web Sites

National Baseball Hall of Fame (www.baseballhalloffame.org). This extensive and highly organized site features, in addition to information on visiting the Hall of Fame and activities there, biographies of all Hall of Fame members.

Robertoclemente21.com (www.robertoclemente21.com). This is the official Roberto Clemente Web site and features a biography, career highlights, photographs, and links to other Clemente sites.

Roberto Clemente Sports City (www.rcsc21.com). Gives the history of *Ciudad Deportiva,* "Sports City," and describes the various programs conducted for young people.

The Baseball Page (www.thebaseballpage.com). An amazingly comprehensive online resource for the baseball fan. Includes player biographies, team histories, statistics, latest news, and much more.

Index